For permissions contact: cheryl@willowtradingsa.co.za

White Fear: Overcoming the Impossible to Get Ahead by **Don MacRobert**

ISBN: 978-0-620-92436-8

1st Edition, Printed in South Africa

Self-Published by Don MacRobert

Cover by: Greg Davies

Editor: Shanna C. Jacobsen

White Fear

Overcoming the Impossible to Get Ahead

Don MacRobert

Grateful Thanks

People said I was crazy to work in Soweto and the truth is, I could not have gone there or into other townships without the wonderful support and loyalty of my wonderful wife, Marianne, and children, Bruce, Cindy, Guy, Nicole, Angus, Duncan and Marcelle.

The family stepped up to the plate—big time.

CONTENTS

Introduction

Thank you for choosing to read this book.

To explain the title, *White Fear*—when I first ventured into Soweto, I was worried about working there. While the worry on my part persistently lingered, this went much deeper, and there was a great deal of fear surrounding my work. This manifested in several ways. It was not blacks' fear of whites, but rather our collective fear of the power of South Africa's apartheid government and the apparatus it used to force draconian laws onto the population.

The story you are about to read is an account of my personal journey during the troubled times of apartheid. These are my views and experiences and do not necessarily reflect the opinions of others. However, many of the situations that I refer to are well documented by academic literature both at the time then, and throughout the course of history.

Foreword

Archbishop Thabo Makgoba

On 25 September 2020, I wrote congratulating Don MacRobert that the Synod of Bishops had resolved the evening before that they had agreed to bestow on him The Order of Simon of Cyrene. This is the highest award by the Anglican Church, and it is bestowed to Laity for Distinguished Service. It is named after Simon of Cyrene, the first African Saint.

The citation, as adopted by all the Bishops, noted his pastoral services, including his working in Soweto for 15 years for Dr Nthato Motlana, and Archbishop Desmond Tutu, for caring for the poor; serving St Alban's College, being the first Anglican school to admit children of colour, and the first school in the country to initiate outreach programmes for students from black schools. He has served as Chancellor for the Diocese of Pretoria, and assisted the Archbishop in piloting a unique method to feed the poor in the squatter camps, by the use of cell phones to deliver food to the poor.

He was recognised for his role as an activist, particularly against the former regime, including visits to prisoners in the high-security section of the Pretoria jail, representing school pupils charged with treason following the 1976 Soweto riots. His service saw his suing the government in a landmark decision involving the environment, and the prevention of illegal cottages on the Wild Coast. He took steps in 1986 to hide 20 pupils from the security police, to enable them to write their matric examinations, successfully.

The above does not include his other activities such as being on the boards of companies quoted on the stock exchange, or being chairman of many organisations such as the National Orchestra, or the SA Ballet, or the National Zoo, or Round Table, and the fact that he was proposed by the late Anton Rupert to serve on the Paris Chamber of Commerce.

The award is not an annual event and other recipients of include the writer Alan Paton, Leah Tutu, Sally Motlana, Saki Macozoma, and Michael Cassidy.

- Archbishop Thabo Makgoba, South African Anglican Archbishop of Cape Town

Acknowledgements

I wondered about writing this book, but I was helped by friends and their interventions

Often, I pondered about the author Margaret Mitchell, who it is said kept her big pile of handwritten manuscripts behind the kitchen door for eight years, only producing them when eventually prompted by friends. She was the author of *Gone with the Wind*. This little book is miles away from that written by Ms Mitchell, but it covers the same actions—Start. Stop. Forget about it. Do nothing. Gather dust.

The germ was planted over 10 years ago by Belinda Sauer who suggested I start recording my experiences of Soweto. She graciously typed up many of the first pages of the anecdotes, then. Thank you, Boxie.

Chris Cowell is a marvellous IT man. He has skills far beyond my ken. Things like cutting, pasting and amendments became a class act

It was Cheryl Uys who picked up a solitary piece of paper and said: "This story needs to be told and fleshed out. Do something!" So, based on her prompting, this little story was elevated from the space behind the kitchen door, where it gathered dust, to this little book.

And I cannot say too much about Shanna Jacobsen. She not only proofed the book, but went further—to check on dates, the introduction of legislation, correcting names of directors. She really kept me on my toes, with many questions, research, probing investigations. Shanna, you were great.

1 ~ Fear

"You are mad!"

Those were the words of a Sowetan himself, Dudley Mekgoe, when he welcomed me to Soweto on my first day.

"You must be afraid!" he cautioned. "Soweto was created out of the worst forms of social engineering that history has ever seen. Soweto is illegitimate—it is a bastard. It has generated hatred and fear," Dudley carried on, without pausing.

My wife, Marianne, and our children wished me Godspeed with whatever I was aiming to do; very supportive, and loyal—always.

And fear? Yes. Loads of it.

Looking over the tightly packed rows of houses, standing shoulder to shoulder with hardly any space in between them, let alone space for a front lawn, were over 250 000 houses cloistered together. The same architectural design for every house—all 250 000 of them. I felt small and helpless in the face of such a creation and its magnitude.

After being elected into power in 1948, the National Party introduced a number of atrocious laws to further keep white South Africans separate from other races, taking far more aggressive measures than the previous regime to enforce apartheid, or separateness. One such measure the government at the time took was shutting down part of Johannesburg known as Sophiatown, removing the black people from here, as well as other areas occupied by blacks; housing them in areas it had created for blacks only, like Soweto, which was established as an artificial suburb in the 1930s.

Old Sophiatown was located in the middle of sprawling Johannesburg, only a few kilometres from the CBD. The problem, as perceived by the government, was that Sophiatown was now quickly becoming home to people of different races. Indeed, it was a flourishing multiracial residential area, complete with bars, or shebeens as they are known locally, almost all illegal and certainly not being registered under any liquor laws. Nonetheless, people brewed their beer and distilled their spirits, and despite the prohibition laws preventing blacks, coloureds and 'other' people from mixing socially with whites, they did so freely.

While this intermingling of races was totally against the government's policy of apartheid, paradoxically, the sequence of events in Sophiatown was purely of the government's own doing.

After mandating that the Johannesburg City Council aggressively enforce an inner-city slum clearance programme, many black people suddenly lost their homes. Having been denied any land ownership permits by the government, they had nowhere to go. At the same time, existing black landowners in Sophiatown, who were within their rights to own their land sold to them by the original landowner, Hermann Tobiansky, faced impossibly large bond repayments. This saw the blacks who were displaced from the city invited to rent land on the properties of black landowners in Sophiatown. Using whatever materials they could find to build their homes, mostly aluminium sheets, it resulted in the expansion of Sophiatown as a shantytown almost overnight, and one that was rapidly encroaching on surrounding white areas.

One of the major irritations of the then government was the fact that black people were entitled, by law, to own their properties in Sophiatown. This meant freehold title for these black property owners. But once the government passed the Natives Resettlement Act in 1954, it meant steps could be taken to close down Sophiatown. And so, the government moved all black people from Sophiatown, as well as other areas it deemed 'necessary', and relocated them to Soweto and other townships.

Naturally, homeowners and residents of Sophiatown resented being moved. They held public meetings. Political leaders such as Nelson Mandela, and many others, spoke to them and gave them moral support—at the very least.

The government's machinery had swung into action. Those living in Sophiatown were physically removed and instead, placed in an area the government had designated for them. Then came the bulldozers. They started flattening people's homes. The remaining few people were forced to gather up their meagre belongings and loaded up onto big trucks that rolled them out to Soweto. All of this had, at its root, the issue of apartheid, which sought to separate races using whatever means possible.

Although it was the National Party that was hellbent on creating and writing a vast array of laws that promoted apartheid, separateness had been long established as a norm in white South Africa, with the first documented use of the Afrikaans word 'apartheid' in 1929. When the National Party was voted into power by the white electorate, apartheid became the central theme of laws passed in Parliament. The National Party stated that its main objective was that of separateness, and by 1950, the title given to this concept of separatism had established itself in everyday life in South Africa.

According to the Nationalist government's legislation process, blacks and whites could not live together. They could not eat together, and restaurants were limited to white people only. If they existed in black areas at all, restaurants could only have black patrons. There were laws prohibiting blacks from holding down jobs; other laws prohibited blacks from attending white universities. Then there were laws prohibiting black people from sitting on benches intended for whites. Post offices had separate entrances, one for blacks and the other for whites. The same for train stations—one entrance for whites and the other for blacks. The whole legal system became flooded with laws aimed at establishing and maintaining its skewed separatist ideals. These laws governed daily lives, from waking up, to transport to work, the work environment, the job one could hold or not hold, where one could eat, or even have a holiday.

Snapshots from South Africa's history books will show that in 1936, the then government enacted the Native Trust and Land Act, which allocated 13% of the country's land for blacks. This was a whoppingly disheartening increase from the previous 7% allocation as per the Natives Land Act of 1913—despite the fact that even then, blacks far outnumbered the white population. When I went to work in Soweto in 1983, there were approximately 22 million blacks in the country and just over 4 million whites; a comparative ratio of roughly five to one. Absolute madness!

Another example of how apartheid was perpetuated is evidenced in the establishment of South Africa's goldmines that provided so much wealth, then, to the stockholders of gold mining companies, and through taxes, to the government of the day. These companies created separate living quarters for black labourers who were regarded as temporary sojourners.

The contract of employment for a black mineworker would last for only 11 months. In the twelfth month, the mineworker was supposed to return to his family. He would leave his family at home, mostly located in a distant rural area, and seek employment on the mines. He became a labourer digging underground and would work in shifts; returning to his sleeping place at the end of each day. This was in a long, low-slung building that housed hundreds of workers. The building would be divided up into large rooms, each sleeping between 10 to 16 labourers. There were never enough dormitories, so they became overcrowded. Rooms were not well-lit, and they certainly were not warm. Often, the men had to sleep bundled up together on limited concrete bunks that even with a mattress and blankets, could not always take away the cold or hardness of the concrete.

These low-slung buildings, or compounds, as they were known, had ablution centres at the end of each block. There were also central areas that doubled as mess halls and kitchens, which, in addition to eating rations provided by the mines, contained sparse facilities where the men could cook their own meals.

And so, it was from the wealth created by the mines that the concept of separate dwellings for blacks was established. White workers on the mines lived in different houses and were usually mine managers or shaft managers. They had their own individual homes with gardens and their positions were secure. Legislation was introduced—ultimately to prevent black people from holding down certain jobs that paid better and were specifically reserved for whites. This gross oppression stifled the lives of so many.

A deplorable piece of social engineering spanning over a long period was the Pass Laws Act. Black people, by law, had to always carry a means of identification. This 'pass' became known as a *dompas*—officially, this was a contraction of the term 'domestic passport' but colloquially, it was a 'dumb pass', and it was an absolute necessity. If ever the police accosted a black person without a pass, it meant immediate imprisonment followed by possible deportation to the person's rural home. This could happen even though the luckless person without their pass had never been to that so-called home for many years, if ever.

The first introduction of these pass laws was as a result of the Stallard Commission established in 1922. Its name was derived from the chairman of the Commission, Colonel C. F. Stallard. He was a well-known churchman, having become chancellor of the Anglican Diocese in Johannesburg. The recommendation of the Stallard Commission was that black people should be obligated to carry a pass. This identification book would record the name of the holder, their race, and in particular, where they were employed. To register as an employee, the employer would have to take the potential employee together with their pass book to the labour offices to have these particulars of employment recorded in the pass book. There were long queues of blacks at the pass offices, all waiting to get their pass books stamped. These passes had to be instantly produced if ever requested by a policeman. The policeman would then carefully scrutinise the documentation to see that the holder had a legitimate job and was entitled to be in a white area. Any mishap or error resulted in the holder being tossed into jail on their way to being deported—imagine being deported from your own land of birth?! There was sometimes the alternative option of paying a fine. However, being at the lowly end of the employment scale with little or no cash available, payment of a fine became almost impossible. Jail life became part of the accepted way of living. Or struggling. And it was in places like Soweto that black people were mandated to live, by law.

Even white women had to ferry their own house servants to the pass office to be registered. Each year, she would drive her car to the pass office, with the black woman servant sitting in the back of the car. That was the accepted norm of conveyance.

Apartheid encapsulated the whole way of life for a black person. While dictating where they could live, this 'living' did not mean that they enjoyed ownership rights to their dwelling or the ground on which it was built. Rather, in 87% of the country where there were jobs, these were reserved for whites and black people could only be temporary dwellers. They would be a tenant but never a landowner.

Similarly, a black person's work or career path was clearly defined. They could become a messenger for a large company; an office cleaner; or a mineworker, down underground in the mines—not a blaster on the mines, or a mine captain, and never someone in top management. There were also laws prohibiting black people from holding any shares in property and construction companies.

Soweto, like many other townships, was built some distance from the city, closer to the industrial areas. White factory owners and manufacturers needed black labour, and it was convenient that Soweto and other black townships were not too far away from the industrial areas. Subsidised transport also meant that it was possible to bus labourers from the townships to the workplace.

With much of Soweto's housing being created in a hurry to accommodate the blacks being forcibly sent there, facilities were shocking. Some of the black townships built closer to other cities, or towns, were better off—they at least had electricity in their homes. This was not so in Soweto, where these homes had to rely on candles, or kerosene lamps. And with no electricity, their stoves had to be fuelled by coal. Without electricity, there could be no heaters or warmers so these stoves, apart from providing a means for cooking, were also the sole source of warmth.

The houses themselves were tiny and called 'matchbox' houses because they were all built exactly the same by the government. Each house consisted of a small living room that would have to double up as the dining room, with two small bedrooms and a kitchen. Ablutions were generally outside in the yard.

A family consisting of two parents with two or three children would all be crammed into the small matchbox home. Parents would sleep in one bedroom, and their children in the other. There were often more than two children. If other members of the family visited, they would be crowded into these tiny living quarters. This was the case when outsiders came to stay—a family member would arrive wanting to find a job, and hence needed accommodation. Or a tragedy may have befallen relatives in a rural area, meaning that the children had to come to town to live with the city dwellers. Everyone would be squashed into that one tiny abode, making it necessary for the children to sleep on the floor under the table in the living or dining room.

The whole area was littered with high-rise security lamps that were electrically driven. These covered a wide area and were designed so that people could be watched from high up to make sure that there was no disturbance. That fear factor was all-pervasive yet, the streets of Soweto became living areas. This was where people of the neighbourhood would meet—and talk. It was this talking that was to play a great role in the evolution of black society. It was the way in which news was passed, and because it was in their vernacular, it could happen safely. This bush telegraph became a reliable source of information, capturing the latest and most important news items then passing the news on quickly, from street to street.

It wasn't until 1976 that there was television in South Africa. This too had been prohibited by the ruling party because of the fear that it might enlighten the people, or show them that some of what was taking place in South Africa was not acceptable in the outside world. The nation was placed in isolation by its own government. It was to be quarantined from outside concepts of liberalism. The Bill of Rights and guarantees of civil liberty were not to be broadcast. The only method of broadcast permitted by the government was the radio, and even these radio stations were monitored and programmed to ensure that the listeners were fed a diet of government propaganda.

Soweto's streets became so important because this was where people could meet; not only for social purposes but also to pass on important news such as political feelings or happenings. This was an alternate or underground channel of information, and the bush telegraph at its finest.

The streets of Soweto were noisy. The matchbox houses crowded each other and because of the non-existent space between each dwelling, any noise in one house could be heard next-door. This noise could be music broadcasting from a radio, or a family having a lively discussion, or even an argument.

Also, in the 1980s, only two main roads in Soweto were tarred—the old Potchefstroom and the Randfontein road, and one, possibly two others.

The rest consisted of dirt or gravel roads. These would become very messy when the summer rains fell, and because of the poor drainage, they would become eroded by rainwater running off them. Roads were bumpy, certainly uneven, and not very good for vehicle transport. At this stage, very few black people owned motorcars. This was because of their jobs, and they just could not afford to buy cars.

For the children of Soweto, the streets were fun. Apart from being the social hub of Soweto, they also became areas for games. Girls would play hopscotch. Boys would play soccer in the dusty streets.

It was also quite common to see a small manufacturer using the street as his factory yard. He would repair shoes, or make furniture using part of the road, but definitely use the sidewalk as his factory area.

In the predawn hours when it was still dark, parents would leave their homes to set off for their work in some distant area. They would have to walk along dusty and uneven streets to find transport to get to work, which meant getting to a train station to catch a train to work. Even the trains were segregated. The third-class coaches, with stark wooden seat benches, were for blacks. White people had the choice to travel in first or second-class coaches. Buses were also used. These would depart from bus terminals taking the workforce to their places of employment, with many of the black women going to work as domestic help in white homes.

Apart from the trains and buses, taxis started becoming important as a means of travel. Originally, when I went to work in Soweto, black people could not own taxi licenses. The early taxi operators started buying big American cars to convey their passengers, mainly the Valiant, originally produced by Plymouth then later Chrysler. They would pack in as many passengers as they could fit. Later, the minibus became popular as a taxi vehicle—it held many more passengers. Even later still, the government introduced legislation allowing the taxis to be legal operators.

Children became integral to black homes. As their parents left for work in the early hours, it was up to the older children in the family to make sure that the younger children were given something to eat before they all left for school. They saw that the younger children were properly dressed in their school uniforms and shepherded to their nearby schools. Most schools in South Africa, including the black schools, have followed the British tradition of having school uniforms—a girl's dress, or tunic, would be of a particular colour and be different from those of another school. The boys, too, had to dress in a standard uniform. Typically, this consisted of long grey trousers (or shorts in summer), a white shirt and a tie. Each school had its own tie.

Having all these uniforms created a great deal of stress in the family because they added considerably to the cost of living.

The work of the children became a necessity because with their parents having gone to work early in the morning and only returning after dark, it was up to the children to start preparing for the evening meal. After returning home from school, they would have to light up the coal stove fires. From four in the afternoon, Soweto's small matchbox houses would start spewing smoke from their chimneys.

If the wind was not blowing the smoke away, it would accumulate into dense smog that would settle over the township. The whole area of Soweto would become enveloped. Everyone was therefore happier when the wind blew in the 'right' direction. But the wind had to blow quite strongly in Soweto. This is because there are no trees in Soweto. Living cheek by jowl, with the houses so close to each other, there was never any space for trees to grow in gardens. In any event, these houses belonged to the government. They were rented and were never owned by its occupants, so why worry about trees?

In the winter months when the wind blew, Soweto became very cold and the windchill factor saw temperatures plummet. The township was serviced by horse-drawn coal wagons driven by a coal merchant who was covered in soot and ash as he journeyed the streets, dropping off enough coal for each family to be used for a week to ignite their fires. I got to know one of these coal merchants—Robert Dluli. He had to work very hard.

Soweto's streets were still busy during the times it was so bitterly cold but people seemed to chat less, unless of course there were matters of great importance, which would be the source of communications systems.

Despite all the difficulties of no electricity and poor infrastructure, Soweto had its own character. Remember, there were no legal or formal structures like school governing bodies, or local municipal ratepayers' associations because there were no land tenure or property rights. Still, its people knew how to deal with hardships, which was clear from their lifestyles. Sowetans became the centre of much political interest and activity. Having been forcibly removed to live in Soweto, the residents were hardened to the laws and practices of the apartheid system—perhaps more hardened than residents of other black townships around the country.

It was the residents of Soweto who showed me in so many ways what resilience was, with my own challenges being a walk in the park compared to theirs! When I told my family I was going to work in Soweto, which white people were prohibited from entering, Marianne's mother who we called 'Ouma', offered some cheerful advice when she said: "I don't know what you are going to do in Soweto, but apart from giving you my blessing, you are always welcome to pop in to see me for coffee and beskuit."

Similar were the words of my very good friend, Virginia Ogilvy Thompson, who said: "Soweto is a no-go area but whatever you are aiming to do, you go with our best blessings."

Thanks to Dudley, I was able to meet so many of the leaders of Soweto. During my time, I met with Jimmy Sojane, the original head of the taxi association, all illegal then. Meanwhile, Lucky Michaels, who was the head of the Taverners Association, oversaw all the illegal shebeens. I also had the pleasure of meeting Kaizer Motaung, the chairman of his self-named soccer club, Kaizer Chiefs, which has one of the biggest support groups around the country, as well as Lekgau 'Tubs' Mathabathe, who was one of the leaders of the 1976 student uprisings. Another notable Sowetan I was fortunate enough to meet was Dr Nthato Motlana, a medical practitioner in Soweto and a firebrand of note—never afraid to speak his mind about the dreadful government and their policies. He was also one of the only specialists who was allowed to visit his patient, Nelson Mandela, held then in the prison on Robben Island, an island 7km off the Cape Town coast and much like the Alcatraz prison in San Francisco Bay. Other people who played a big part in my career in Soweto included Advocate Dikgang Moseneke; and as he was then, Bishop Desmond Tutu.

2 ~ Get Ahead Foundation

I was touched by the warm send-off given to me by Monty Knoll, former Chairman of the Association of Law Societies' Editorial Committee. I had just left the law practice and against this backdrop, accepted the challenge of working in Soweto. Monty clearly didn't know what I was going to do in Soweto and being launched into the unknown, I didn't have a clear idea of this either.

The aim was to set up a company. It was Colin Hall who flighted the idea of starting a company in Soweto, with me to become its chief executive officer. The idea was to form a big public company then sell shares, but only to blacks. This would make it an all-black-owned company. There would be no white shareholders at all. Our dream was to make the company, once formed with shareholders, into a large dynamic organisation. It would have factories. Maybe these factories could make cigarettes, or clothing. If that time in Soweto showed me anything, it's that black people love clothing and are very brand conscious and fashion-forward. Even back then, with not much money, they knew the best brand for shirts, or shoes. Shoes became especially important because people had to walk a long way from their homes in the townships to the bus stop or taxi rank or train station, therefore, shoe comfort became a much-discussed point. Blacks knew the very best brands for shoes. I remember Florsheim being bandied about as *the* brand for best shoes. I had never heard of this brand but checked in a few stores, and sure enough, there they were.

There were also skippers—skippers had become the popularly accepted name for t-shirts in Soweto. The name was derived from a retail outlet that popularised the sale of t-shirts: Skipper Bar. That was the place that you bought these t-shirts, or skippers.

We felt that this public company of ours would quickly grow in shareholding numbers, which would lead to making more capital available. With this capital, we could have money to not only have factories to make our own fashion goods, but also have a chain of retail stores.

What a lovely success story it would be—it was black economic empowerment in the making. And all in the face of a fearful and threatening white government.

Colin had even persuaded three big listed companies to support us by paying a quarterly sponsorship. Those three companies were United Tobacco Company, where Bruce Edmunds was the CEO; Premier Milling, where Tony Bloom was the CEO; and John Newbury from Nissan. I felt elated. I was playing with the big guys.

This led to us having a magnificent launch at the swish Carlton Hotel in downtown Johannesburg. The Carlton was a splendid venue and was a meeting place, and if ever you wanted to find any Secretary of State, cabinet minister or big business mogul, that was the place to look.

We had this magnificent launch attended by over 300 black people. We encouraged them to buy shares in our company called Get Ahead Limited. Colin had liked the word 'ahead' but it needed a qualifying name. What about 'get', I offered, to make it 'Get Ahead'. The name stuck. We told the people that the sale of the shares would ultimately benefit them.

Then Dudley asked something strange. "Of course, you do know that the Special Branch will be at the launch, as well?"

"How can that be?!" I asked Dudley, adding that, "Surely Colin and I are to be the only white people in the audience?"

Not so, he continued.

The security police—a unit of the South African Police Service also known as the Special Branch—were everywhere, and they would definitely attend an event with a large turnout of blacks in downtown Johannesburg, which was a white area. These guys looked like us; they dressed quietly, no big, brash showing off; and they would be sitting wired up, near the microphone so that they can tape all the proceedings—especially when Dr Motlana got up to speak about the government's racist laws militated against blacks. They waved their hands as if they were clapping, but they did not emit any sound so as not to interfere with the sound recording systems wired to them.

Whew! Here comes that thought again—fear.

Alarmingly, there wasn't a mad rush on the night of the launch to buy shares. People certainly took home the share subscription forms. They said they would call us—more along the lines of "don't call us, we'll call you", and to our surprise, we heard very little back. We could not believe that people could be so slow on the uptake. We expected a rush of subscribers. Possibly a stampede. Alas, this was not to be.

We decided to do some follow up calls. This produced a few new subscribers. Some people did start buying shares in Get Ahead Limited.

Sadly, because of the past racist laws of the country, people did not understand quite what we were offering. They could not understand the concept of holding shares in a company, let alone a company aiming to be listed on the stock exchange. This was because some of the laws had previously prohibited black people from holding shares in companies. Now, all of a sudden, they were asked to do something which had previously been prohibited to them. This was something very new—too new. At one of the meetings, I heard one of the attendees saying that what we were trying to do was to sell insurance. We were like an insurance company. If people die, there would be certain benefits for their families.

This was not the case at all, but it somehow persuaded a few more people to join. To try and avoid misleading people, we had to have a covering memorandum explaining what the company was all about; and that our company was registered at the Companies Office in Pretoria. It would be agreed that by paying a minimum of R100, the applicant could become a shareholder in our company, once the application form had been processed and registered.

To try and increase sales of shares, we decided to start holding meetings in Soweto. We invited not just people who we thought were leaders and entrepreneurs but also, ordinary residents.

It was a very slow process. We received support from one of the better-known associations, the Black Chamber of Commerce, known as the National African Federated Chamber of Commerce (NAFCOC). They had a dynamic president, Dr Sam Motsuenyane. He was incredibly supportive and encouraged any activity that would work to promote black entrepreneurship. He often came to address meetings where we were aiming to pitch to the public to buy shares. He would give us full support. Sam told us that this was the start of black economic empowerment. We must hang in there even if the sale of shares was proving to be difficult. Despite Sam's encouragement, there was no mad rush as we had hoped. Rather, this was turning out to be a long, slow slog.

During meetings in Soweto, we would address residents telling them all about the advantages of becoming shareholders in the company. They would hold share certificates. They would earn dividends. This should help them gain wealth.

We had set ourselves a target of a thousand shareholders. At the end of the spectacular launch at the Carlton Hotel, we had about a hundred shareholders. Thereafter, week by week, we would get a few further completed shareholder subscription forms. But it would be necessary to arrange new and further meetings with new potential shareholders. While trying to follow up on the previous audiences, it was necessary to spread the word. We had to reach out to more people. We needed more shareholders.

It was a real struggle, and despite our optimism, the results were not at all good.

During all this time, we were very lucky to have Nissan Motor Company, Premier Milling and United Tobacco Company sponsor us. Contributions from these corporate donors enabled us to pay the meagre salaries of Dudley, and newcomers Peter Magano and Djundju Mathibe—both formerly from Robben Island prison. I was able to draw a little bit of income now and then, and Marianne and the children continued to be marvellous in their support.

Should any of the sponsors have been a bit slow in making these quarterly payments, we were up against the wall to pay our month-end salaries. Things were very tight. Fortunately, our sponsors were very good, but there were times when we sweated it out.

As time went by, we realised that we were not on a winning ticket. Not many people came to our meetings at which we were trying to introduce the company and sell shares.

The sale of shares dried up to a mere trickle.

We were now at our wits' end and didn't know what to do or how to proceed. The realisation that at this rate, we were not going to be a success at all was crushing, and I was ready to throw in the towel. I would have to go back to a law practice in white South Africa. What would I say to Marianne and the children?

My nose would really be out of joint. How could I, as a former President of the Chamber of Commerce in Pretoria, be so unsuccessful? Surely, I must have been the answer to black economic woes. The unemployment figures among black people were a grave concern. Politically, they were downtrodden. Here, at least, was real hope. It was an economic opportunity. And yet, we were a dismal failure.

Then, Dudley suggested that we meet with Desmond Tutu. At that stage, he was still a Bishop but well on his way to stepping into the role of Archbishop. He was the General Secretary of the South African Council of Churches and a vocal figurehead when it came to the oppression of black people. His office was in downtown Johannesburg. Dudley and I went to see him. We told him what we had been trying to do. We explained that the dream was black economic advancement and empowerment. We thought that the best way would be to create this big company owned by blacks, with lots of black shareholders. We honestly believed that there would be thousands of shareholders, not the mere hundred that we had achieved. We sought his advice. Bishop Tutu was fantastic. He suggested that we should not aim to create capitalists in the form of shareholders in public companies and we should rather aim to create jobs for those who were unemployed in Soweto.

At the time, hundreds of thousands of black people were unemployed in South Africa. These people needed to generate some form of income to feed their families, as well as educate their children. The Bishop doubted whether the creation of a few thousand shareholders could bring relief to all the impoverished, unemployed and poor people of Soweto.

As a result of these discussions, we set out on a completely new tack. We decided to set up a new company, a not-for-profit company that we called Get Ahead Foundation. The name "Get Ahead" had aspirational overtones. It captured the mood of what black people wanted. They wanted to uplift themselves. They wanted to get ahead. As a not-for-profit company, the Get Ahead Foundation would not have shareholders. There would be no dividends. There would be no capital growth. This new company stimulated a mindset of lifting oneself upwards economically. That was what black people really needed.

The new Get Ahead Foundation was to be one of the forerunners of the non-governmental organisation (NGO) movement in South Africa and its objectives were fleshed out with Bishop Tutu. He said that we should aim to create jobs and employment opportunities among the poorest of the poor. The unbanked and so-called 'unbankable'. These became our main objectives.

To achieve these objectives, we had to start raising money. We could not rely on shareholders as in the old company; because we had now set up a not-for-profit NGO. We would have to rely on new donor funding, and this would unfortunately mean we had to part ways with our three sponsors.

To carry out our goal of creating jobs through the Get Ahead Foundation, we realised the first thing required by a start-up venture capitalist was capital, or money. This would enable people to start their own businesses. But black people could not borrow money. They certainly could not loan money from the banks because they had nothing to offer as collateral security for a loan. A black person could not own property in Soweto, or virtually in the entire South Africa. This was because of the laws that meant blacks had to live on 13% of the land—far away from cities where there were jobs. But black people could not live in white areas unless they stayed as temporary residents in the townships that had been 'specially' created for them. In townships like Soweto, a black person was merely a tenant and paid a monthly rental fee to the municipality. Not owning the property, a borrower could not offer the property as security or collateral for a loan.

Then again, hardly any blacks had any other assets to offer. Most were employees in large companies or factories, or at white homes. They were paid wages for the work which they were doing, as labourers in most cases. They had very little extra or disposable income to acquire other assets that could then be used as security for a bank loan.

Very few people in Soweto were able to own a motorcar. Everybody relied on public transport such as the buses, or trains; more recently, they started relying on the informal taxis, which had shown remarkable growth, but the bottom line from a realistic and commercial point of view was that black people did not have any assets to offer a bank as collateral for a loan.

There were a great many people in Soweto who were unemployed. Speculation was that the unemployment figure was between 25% and 30% of its workforce. This was extraordinarily high, by any measure.

That was why Get Ahead set out to help the unemployed. We wanted to empower these people by helping them set up their own small businesses. We were aiming at the informal cottage industries. People who might be sewing, or knitting. While others might be embarking on beadwork, or home cooking to sell the food along the wayside. Men were encouraged to become involved in carpentry or welding. Automotive repairs were also starting to become important as more people slowly started acquiring the means to purchase cars. Quite a few people in Soweto had worked in the motor industry, often as mechanics or learner mechanics and they had a useful basic knowledge of motorcars. They were able to start up their own small businesses in Soweto repairing vehicles and some of them became quite skilled.

It was almost impossible for these budding entrepreneurs to start their businesses on their own. They could not raise a loan or sufficient capital to buy basic equipment such as a sewing machine, or lathes for carpentry. Something had to be done.

With the encouragement of Bishop Tutu, we decided we had to start raising some money that would be loaned to these aspirant businesspeople.

We came to an agreement with our three original sponsors that their sponsorship would come to an end, and that a small portion of the money they had given us could be used as start-up capital for these budding informal entrepreneurs.

And so, we launched our lending programme in Soweto.

Most of the people who we loaned money were illiterate or at best, semi-literate. The fact that they could hardly read did not mean they were not gung-ho about wanting to start their own small businesses. And savvy! We were immensely encouraged that we found a huge crop of would-be capitalists.

Their inability to read or write meant that they could not follow any legal loan contract that might be placed before them because they would not understand its meaning or contractual obligations. More specifically, they could also not really sign their names to a contract., other than marking it with the letter 'X'.

Slowly we started evolving our own lending rules. We found that peer pressure was our most useful tool, or mechanism, to ensure loans were repaid timeously.

The process worked like this: if we loaned money to Agnes to help her start her sewing business and she was a bit slow in paying back, we would follow an interesting route. When Beatrice came to look for a loan, we would say to her, "Yes, we want to lend you money for your knitting business, but Agnes has yet to pay us back. You go and chase Agnes. When she pays us, we can then lend you the money." The same when Cynthia came to borrow money for a cooking business. We would tell Cynthia to join Beatrice and chase Agnes together. Peer pressure would set in and our money would pop back. We were then in a position to start lending money to Beatrice, or the next in line. This worked marvels; the loan was repaid—and fairly promptly.

We followed the principle of groups being organised into *stokvels*. These 'gatherings' became a way of financial dealing, especially among women. Ten women, say, would come together to form a group. Each month, all the women would put money into the pot, or kitty, and if each person contributed R200, the total monthly subscription would come to R2 000. In strict rotational order, the first lady would take the whole pot of R2 000. This bigger amount could then pay for her children's school fees that month, or school uniforms. Or be a down payment for a new sewing machine.

Next month, the stokvel group would meet again, with each person paying that same monthly contribution of R200 into the pot so that the second person on the list would receive the next amount of R2 000.

There were very strict rules. Nobody could withdraw from the group until each rotational payment dividend had been paid out to all members. The peer pressure to repay was huge. On the advice of the United States Agency for International Development (USAID), we followed the principles of Grameen Bank in Bangladesh by using group pressure to encourage borrowers to repay the loans.

One day, I took a well-known mining magnate on a tour of Soweto. I used to take many people on such tours. This was to introduce them to our work and the small businesses we were trying to grow. I explained to our visitor this peer pressure of Beatrice and Cynthia chasing Agnes to make her repay her loan so that they in turn could get their loans. The magnate was dismayed. He said to me we were acting as a sort of banker. He mentioned that no banker would disclose the financial affairs of one customer to another, or yet to a third customer, or fourth. I agreed but mentioned that the banks were not operating in Soweto. Black people could not get loans. They had no collateral security to offer, so we had to develop our own rules.

At this time, it was also very difficult for a small business person to get started. There was so much red tape. The problem became more acute if you were black. There were laws that prohibited blacks from having certain occupations; or doing certain work. Specific jobs were reserved for whites. Blacks could not enter the formal job market all that easily.

To get around this red tape, we suggested to our borrowers and would-be capitalists: start trading. Start your dressmaking business in your home. Repair motor cars. If you have to have increased space for your work, use the pavement outside your house. And this is what the people did.

During the tour with the mining magnate, he also asked me if the small businesspeople obtained licenses to trade. I told him that was not so. We merely encouraged them to start without going through the whole red tape rigmarole of trying to get a license. He again expressed surprise that we could trade illegally. He wondered how people could start trading without obtaining a license I explained that to obtain a license required so much red tape and rigmarole. This was difficult for any small business person to understand. When it came to illiterate or semiliterate people it was a complete non-starter.

Most people who had their own businesses and had the entrepreneurial flame to get started on their own, would appreciate what we were doing. I remember meeting the late Dr Anton Rupert, himself a pioneer in the South African business scene. He was later to float many public companies in South Africa and then take them offshore for listing in places such as Switzerland and England. He was very excited about what we were trying to do. His eyes lit up when we showed him photographs of small traders with their carpentry businesses. He smiled when we showed him a shopkeeper who had converted a tiny garage into a shop with shelves and a counter. He was not particularly concerned that not all our start-up businesses were trading according to the strict letter of the law. He thought it was exciting that so many people could be helped to get that first step up the economic ladder.

This was not always going to be the case with large South African businesses. There were some who played it by the book, to a fault. If ever I asked them for funding to support our small venture, they would question me rigorously and ask what would stop me from also adopting a slightly illegal role, insinuating that I might be tempted to put my own hands in the till. In this way, I would also be breaking the law and just be the same as the illegal small traders.

Fortunately, a good friend, Lin Anderson came to my aid. She had been a well-known columnist on the *Rand Daily Mail*, an opposition newspaper which, sadly, had closed down. After closing down, Lin started her own small lending programme. This was called the Get Up Trust. It also proved to be successful.

Lin said that I should not worry about those industrialists who challenged me about breaking the laws to help so many people get started in business. Why would I take money? That was theft!

Lin explained that the laws which I had targeted, and were breaking, were morally unjustified. It was morally incorrect for black people to be denied the right to trade in certain areas; or the right to have certain jobs; or to have economic freedom, in general. Once we had clearly identified the offending laws, Lin encouraged me to break them wholesale, and our 'illegal', but morally just acts, continued.

To be in a position to lend money to the small entrepreneurs, we needed to raise more funds. This was a real struggle to begin with.

This was when Bishop Tutu came to the fore. Big time. He gave me a letter of introduction and support. I was to use this letter in the United States of America. That introduction got us very far.

Armed with this letter from Bishop Tutu, I flew to New York. One of my first meetings was with the Episcopal Church of 2nd Avenue, New York. There I met a lovely lady, Nan Marvel. I explained to Nan what we were trying to do. I mentioned the huge unemployment rate. I told her that many people were hanging around Soweto with nothing to do. This could be a tinder box. People would revolt for want of money or food.

I mentioned that the women of Soweto, and other black townships, were tough. They knew about hardship. I told Nan about Mrs Chauke roasting her corn on the cob, called *mielies*. She was one of the first people to receive a loan from the money sent from New York, by Nan Marvel of the Episcopalian denomination.

I met Mrs Chauke at her little stall next to the Mamelodi train station—a busy station. So many people had to walk from their small non-electrified matchbox houses, and they would catch a train from the Mamelodi station to take them to work in town, or to the industrial sites where the factories were situated. But those stations then were not like Liverpool Street Station in London, or Grand Central in New York. Those stations only had a ticket office, where you bought your train ticket, and a toilet facility of sorts for men and women. There was no food establishment or bookstore, or waiting lounge or sitting room. Shops like Saks of New York, or Smiths Stationers, were out of the question.

Mrs Chauke was smart. She was a very hard worker. Not having any McDonalds or Starbucks at the railway station, she sold her roasted *mielies*. Her oven was a charcoal-filled brazier filled almost to the top with embers. The brazier was an old oil can with holes punched into the side to give air to the red glowing embers. On top of the glowing coals, she had wire netting that she used to roast the *mielies*. She sat on a small chair next to her oven. People catching trains would stop momentarily at her stall, grab a warm mielie, and hurry to the platform. That was their meal before getting to work.

The main traffic flow was in the early morning from about 6.00am until about 8.00am, and it was very cold and dark in winter. It then got quieter, only to get busy in the afternoons when the stampede of home goers would descend from about 4.00pm until 7.00pm and it would get cold, again, and dark.

Mrs Chauke sat in the cold in the early mornings, and in the cold in the evenings. No cover, no canopy. Shivering if it was raining and boiling hot by midday when the sun was at its peak. She was able to earn enough money to feed her children and pay their school fees. A hard-working woman. I thought about the words: driven, determined, mother, warm.

Peter and I asked her if we could help her with her business. We might be able to lend some money, if it would help. But she had to understand that she had to repay the loan. No baulking or missed instalments. That was an absolute condition. However, if she paid on time, she could then borrow for a second time, then a third, and so on.

Peter and Mrs Chauke worked out her cashflow; her take-home pay; her requirements for her children, and how much she could pay back against her outstanding loan. Of course, any similar business person does the same.

The first loan would be used to get her a cover, like a big umbrella, to shield against the elements. The second loan purchased another coal brazier to almost double her takings, or turnover. The business started getting traction.

And after repaying the first and second loans, Mrs Chauke asked for a third loan to enable her to buy more of her raw product—*mielies*.

The amounts we are talking about for each loan, with all the calculations for the loan, then the repayment, future earnings and savings, was US$5, or in local terms, R25. That's all. It is amazing that with these small loans, we were able to assist the people at the bottom of the ladder.

I was very excited to write to Nan Marvel in 2nd Avenue, New York, to give her a progress report, with photographs. She had bought into my proposal almost immediately. It was thanks to her that we got our first big grant. This was $50 000. A tremendous amount of money when you realise that at the time, the exchange rate of $1 was equal to R5. At that stage, most of our loans to the emerging entrepreneurs were between R100 and R500. Not great amounts of money yet, they were able to provide the wherewithal to the borrowers to buy their first equipment such as the sewing machine, or materials to make dresses, or wood for a carpentry business.

$50 000 went a long way. We were able to swing into action immediately in Soweto. We then took our programme to Atteridgeville—a township outside Pretoria. We settled on Atteridgeville because Peter knew this area well from his pre-Robben Island days of canvassing for supporters for the then-banned African National Congress (ANC).

Soon, we were able to take photographs of these budding entrepreneurs. They were bricklayers; welders; carpenters; seamstresses. We kept photographs of these small businesses in a plastic folder that we would show to potential donors. More often than not, they, like Dr Anton Rupert, would smile.

But Bishop Tutu went further. Those stories follow…

3 ~ 1959

The frightening thing about all the apartheid laws was how they impacted so many underprivileged people, in all walks of life. Whether it was in the job market, where laws dictated that blacks could only work at designated lower levels and were disqualified from holding the more important positions, or where you had to live—such as in the black townships like Soweto. Black people were also not allowed to move from one location to another.

My first direct encounter with apartheid came in the field of education when I was 19 years old. I was studying law at the University of Cape Town (UCT) when I came face to face with the government's intention to convert all existing universities to whites-only academic institutions. The government proposed in 1959 that all blacks had to enrol at new university institutions, designated for blacks only. As a newly elected member of the UCT Student Representative Council (SRC), I knew I had to do something to voice my opposition.

Come to think of it, my parents had ensured that we three children enjoyed sheltered early lives. One of my earliest recollections was when our father returned to Pretoria upon the cessation of World War II. He had been away fighting in Egypt. When he returned after spending five years in the war, he had to start earning an income again. He rejoined his father's law firm during a time when the economic situation after the war was in dire straits. The economy had collapsed. There were no bus services reaching our home area. That meant that we had to share transport as my parents had only one motor car between them. This led to my father and two other businesspeople starting a lift club, where he would use his car to collect the other two business colleagues on one day, leaving their wives the use of their cars to be able to go shopping, or to run other errands.

Similarly, with the tough economic situation, my mother had bought an old Singer treadle sewing machine, not electric. She made many of our clothes. She cooked for us. She taught us to read from a wide array of books and encyclopaedias. I was brought up on a diet of books covering a range of subjects. I loved the stories of the big explorers and adventurers. People like Captain Robert Falcon Scott, the UK Royal Navy officer who conducted expeditions to Antarctica only to fall a few miles from his home base. Or the many explorers who ventured into the middle of Africa; people like Livingstone, Speke, and many others. Imagine Livingstone leaving Kuruman in the Northern Cape, and heading into Africa—no roads, only ox wagons not knowing if there would be food or water? He didn't know what to expect. The unknown.

It was a big day for us all when my mother bought a very tired, second-hand Austin car for herself. That gave her wheels!

My father loved playing the piano. He was a gifted musician and would pick up almost any tune to entertain others and us children. His musical talent passed me by, for the most part, and I seem to have missed out on this at a performance level. My brother could sing and play the guitar very well, although my sister was the best, studying music at UCT and then in London. She inherited my father's musical talent, and his ear, including his ability to pounce onto any piece of music and play it almost immediately.

Living close to a golf and tennis club, my parents used to frequent the country club on a regular basis. Apart from playing a good game of tennis, my mother excelled at golf, winning many trophies. An even better golf player was my uncle Mello MacRobert, having played off a scratch handicap for years. The caddies at the golf club were young black teenagers. Many had dropped out of formal education in order to earn a living. One such caddy was a black teenager named Geoff Mphakati. He lived in another black township outside Pretoria, known as Mamelodi. He loved my mother and would pop over to our house every now and again. He was older than me by about 10 years. We would play ball games. But in particular, as a young boy, he taught me the words and tune of a wonderful song, or hymn, sung by the Xhosa people called *Nkosi Sikelel' iAfrika*. Little did I know that the hymn would later become part of our national anthem! After his release from prison, Nelson Mandela played a key role in getting that song to form part of our national anthem.

My schooling was a happy one. Firstly, at the Waterkloof House Preparatory School run by another uncle, Wilfred MacRobert and his wife, Marion. They introduced us to their way of political thinking, that of being liberals and further left than the established white political parties. I enjoyed my later high school years at Michaelhouse in what is today KwaZulu-Natal, where my school reports didn't heap huge amounts of praise on me, apart from my singing in the operettas, in the Gilbert and Sullivan plays.

I was very excited when a rogue radio station started broadcasting, illegally, in 1956, every Sunday evening at 7.00pm. They started each performance by playing the well-known opening bars of Beethoven's 5th Symphony. Apparently, with Pretoria having a number of hills surrounding it, the pirates would broadcast from the top of a hill and quickly scuttle away to avoid getting caught by the Special Branch police. They were never caught but rumours suggested that they were from the small Liberal Party, which included my uncle Wilfred, and Marion, as well as Tony and Johnny Brink, Colin Lang, and others. The illegal use of certain radio frequencies certainly got the juices going!

I loved the University of Cape Town (UCT), immensely. The academic latitude, and the wide variety of views and social interaction with people of colour who had better brainpower and understanding than I did, was marvellous. I was lucky to share accommodation with very good friends. Those were happy days, filled with much fun and laughter. One of my closest friends was Malcolm Douglas. He too was a political animal, interested in the political landscape. He joined me in 1958 when I offered to do door-to-door canvassing for the opposition party, the United Party. We were allocated a poor white area close to the Cape Flats. Not one of them supported the United Party, and they all voted for the ruling National Party. I felt sad for these poor people until Malcolm reminded me that they at least had the vote.

At about the same time, in 1959, parliamentary structures saw the National Party in the overwhelming majority. They strongly advocated the apartheid policy. The United Party opposition was fragmented when five of its members broke away to form a small splinter group, calling themselves the Progressive Party. Unlike the other main parties, they introduced—for the first time ever—a vote that would be given to blacks who had the assets and financial muscle to qualify. They were welcomed with scorn by the other main political parties. All the brave Ministers of Parliament who formed the Progressive Party lost their seats in the next election held in 1961. Apart from one member, Helen Suzman, a fiery and forthright lady. She took no nonsense, giving the ruling Nationalists a terrible time with her ascorbic humour and prying mind. She was to remain in Parliament for the next 13 years as the sole member of her opposition party. And she gave them hell! One woman, against 220 men in their black suits. Helen Suzman would go on to stay in Parliament for many more years.

I decided to become elected to the UCT's student representative council, or the SRC. This was a vocal and militant group strongly opposed to the Nationalist regime and its policies. In 1959, the National Party took their apartheid vision even further. They introduced a new Bill, known as the Extension of University Education Act, Act 45 of 1959. The Act aimed to separate tertiary education institutions by race and deemed it a criminal offence for a non-white person to be registered at a university without the written permission of the Minister of Internal Affairs. So, it became a criminal offence to study at a so-called white university without the necessary permission, which, in later practice, was hardly ever granted. Imagine going to jail because you wanted to study further?

This led to my participating in student meetings and protests with placards shouting abuse at the government. Wearing our black academic gowns in silent student vigils outside the Houses of Parliament. Cold water being thrown over us from a small car containing opposition students.

Through these protests, I came to meet other student leaders. Friends like Jonty Driver and Hugh Lewin. They were amazing in leading the protests and shouting down the government. More than that, they went to jail for sabotage. They had blown up pylons carrying electricity. The government finally allowed both Hugh and Jonty to leave jail and the country, on what was known as an exile permit. In return, they would sign a document stating that they would never return to South Africa. They were banished from their country of birth and upbringing. Helen Suzman helped me to complete Hugh's exile permit application.

4 ~ Security Prison

During my time at the law firm, Adams & Adams, where my uncle Mello MacRobert was chairman and I was the youngest and by far, the most junior of the partners, I got talking with Bill Schuurman—the only other junior partner. We were deeply disturbed by the Nationalist government's most recent law that enforced detention without trial. We felt we must do something. We thought we could add weight to the opposition.

It was a very brave, very stupid notion—a forlorn, losing cause.

It was late 1971. There were only 12 partners in the law firm then. I sat at the bottom end of the table. Small fry.

Then Jan Steyn, a senior partner, got me into a corner. I was previously asked to join a three-man delegation to attend my first ever International Patent Conference (AIPPI) in Mexico City, at the age of 31. While at the event, Jan would attend all the meetings and plenaries, taking stacks of notes. He would explain to clients the intricacies of patent laws, like extensions of time, novelty and examination. He was very clever. Meanwhile, I was tasked with the job of scouring the coffee shops and bars, giving handshakes to clients—especially potential clients. My objective was to gain more clients for the firm. They used to call it 'touting', which was considered an offence in those days!

Jan was a political animal, and astute. He was the son of Colin Steyn who had been the Minister of Justice in Prime Minister Jan Smuts' cabinet, and the grandson of President Steyn, a former president of the old Boer republic, the Orange Free State. Jan was appointed chairman of the United Party's Northern Transvaal branch. The UP came about as a result of the merge between the South African Party and the Union Party. Until its dissolution in the 1970s, anyone who was either part of the ruling Nationalist government's opposition or in support of it, was called a *bloedsap*, or blood sap, with the S, A and P being a reference to its South African Party roots.

According to the way in which Jan saw the situation, it was easy. He told me that I should resign from law and go do my bit for politics—or practice properly as a patent attorney and do so with gusto. His words still ring in my ears.

"Mannetjie, jy het te veel kinders. Moenie mal wees nie!" (Little man, you have too many children. Don't be mad!)

So that was that. I stayed at the law practice, but that very brave, very stupid notion never quite left me.

By then, Mello had also become Chairman of the Progressive Party for the Northern Transvaal, where Pretoria, its capital, was situated. It was a tiny party in 1971 with only one Member of Parliament from 1959 until 1974. That member was the very brave and courageous Helen Suzman—a remarkable lady and a very good friend of Mello.

One morning, my office telephone rang. *"Meneer. Speursersant Visagie hier van die veiligheidspolisie. Jy ken Hugh Lewin. Hy wil jou sien. Kom na die tronk in Potgieter Straat."* (Mister. Detective Sergeant Visagie here, from the security police. You know Hugh Lewin. He wants to meet you. Come to the jail on Potgieter Street).

I nearly fell off my chair. The fear that the Special Branch instilled into a person was unbelievable. They would follow suspects in unlicensed cars and tapped people's telephones without any court order. They intercepted mail addressed to you by steaming off the gum on letters and resealing them with glue. It was very unnerving to be under their scrutiny. They arrested people on a whim of suspicion. The fear was real and staring me in my face.

The main jail in Pretoria was in Potgieter Street. It had a high-security section there for white political prisoners only. Black political prisoners were sent to Robben Island. I was summoned to where Hugh was being held.

Despite my fear, by this time, I had resolved in my little head to do something in the political space.

Long before the advent of computers and emails, much of the workflow processes at Adams & Adams relied on post. The postal service was very efficient then. Letters mailed from New York on a Thursday would arrive on Monday in Pretoria; letters sent from London on Friday would also arrive on Monday, so the Monday post was big, and bulky, tapering off by Wednesday, with another build-up towards the weekend. Patent post went to Jan Steyn to distribute among us patent partners while trademark post was delivered to the Head of Department, Gustav Visser. Gustav was not qualified as an attorney. He and Gordon Wegger had qualified under an old grandfather clause under the Companies Act as company practitioners. It meant Gustav could practice as a practitioner and sign trademark applications. When the post arrived, he would telephone Brendan Somerville and Jasper Vlok and they would stand next to him as he slowly sorted through the mail. He would offer comments: "That Geoff Webster has a cheek", and "what does Marcel Deschamps (of Langner Parry, New York) want now?!"

Geoff Webster was smart. He offered good consultancies to Gustav and Gordon, especially as the latter had just landed the trademark work from Rembrandt's Distillers Corporation. In subsequent years, Geoff's firm would benefit substantially from this.

With the pace of work being what it was at Adams & Adams, Wednesday mornings were quieter. I resolved then to try do a little bit for human rights each Wednesday morning, not quite knowing where to start.

Thursday evenings were bridge night at the Pretoria Country Club and where I would meet up with Bill Schuurman, Peter Good and Willem du Plessis. We might have represented a local mix with two UP supporters, one Nationalist, and a Progressive, or Prog—me. Because of the stormy political scene at the time, it was agreed that we would play until 10.00pm and go home, and NO politics. Our wives agreed to that condition.

Generally, things went well, until Peter asked Willem one evening how the Nat government could justify detention without trial. Well, that was the end of the bridge game. The argument would rage on. Then, being in the days before cell phones, the payphone downstairs would start ringing. Esmé du Plessis, Willem's wife, would be calling. She is a very clever lady. I was still studying for my bar exams in London when Mello wrote that she was the first-ever lady to be admitted as a patent agent. He recruited her from Hahn & Hahn and would often shout at her down the corridor: "Es!" Es was what he called her. "Es, I need your opinion on…"

He valued her opinion enormously. So, after Esmé called late that night, that was the end of the game—long after midnight and well past that original time of 10.00pm.

When I arrived at the jail to see Hugh, I was escorted by Detective Sergeant Visagie of the Special Branch who took me inside, opening and clanging big gates as we progressed deeper in the dungeon with a huge bunch of keys swinging at his side. Eventually, he led me into a room with a small window or hatch. I was told to wait. I was terrified. Cold shivers ran up my spine. Would they let me out?

Eventually, Hugh arrived in the next room. He signalled that I was to speak to him through the hatch, but he intimated that our conversation would be recorded and to not say anything which could implicate me. He didn't need to warn me because I was shivering in my boots! Hugh explained that some of his fellow inmates had been represented by the likes of George Bizos; Sydney Kentridge, who later received a knighthood and the title of Sir; Arthur Chaskalson; and David Soggott—all the big lawyers, but they were all from Johannesburg. The prisoners needed someone from Pretoria, mainly for admin matters like insurance, gifts and so on. I agreed. But then he asked: "You realise that you're now a marked and listed person?" Still shivering, I acknowledged my situation.

He asked if others could approach me. Over time at the jail, I saw incarcerated people like John Laredo, Fred Carneson, and others. Once, I saw Bram Fischer, who, as a top Oxford-educated lawyer, had decided to join the struggle.

When Hugh wanted to leave South Africa, I applied for his exile permit through the offices of Helen Suzman, where an applicant would agree to leave South Africa forever, and never be permitted to return.

I was so frightened that I never told any of our partners, including Chairman Mello MacRobert. I went on my merry way not ever telling anyone at the firm. Nobody. Fear is indeed a formidable foe. I thought no-one knew, until one day, at a partners' meeting with me sitting at the far end of the table—the most junior in the 12-person partnership—Jasper Vlok said: "Mr Chairman, one of our partners is visiting the political prisoners at the high-security section of the Pretoria jail."

Mello exclaimed: "What?! Unbelievable! Which of our partners is doing that?!"

My stomach, brain, and heart collapsed. Now comes trouble. Heaps of it.

Slowly my hand went up. "It's me," I said, very quietly.

Now comes more trouble. With a capital 'T' for Trouble. Imagine the scorn.

Jasper went on to explain that he had received a call from General Motors in Chicago. They were pleased to learn of our efforts in the political section of the prison. They had been told by Buller Pagden, the Chairman of Pagdens law firm in Port Elizabeth and the attorneys for General Motors in South Africa. His sister-in-law, Liz Pitman, was married to Hugh. The word was out via another bush telegraph of sorts.

As we left the partners meeting, still trembling like a leaf, Jan Steyn and the others gave me a clap on the back.

5 ~ 1976

I had thought that my close calls with the Special Branch had come to a halt. But that was not the case.

During a visit with Hugh at the Pretoria jail, I recalled his words: "Please see if there is anything that can be done for the schoolchildren in the black townships." Those words stayed with me, and so, in early 1975, I made a date to meet Mr Samuel John Sedise Moseneke, a prominent educator in the Atteridgeville township, just outside Pretoria. He was a fine gentleman.

I drove to see him at his home in Atteridgeville. Apart from the purpose of the meeting, he mentioned that his two boys, Dikgang, and Tiego, were both in prison at the call of the government for their anti-apartheid activities. He also mentioned his dream of one day building his retirement home in Mabopane, north of Pretoria, which he eventually did.

My goal was to find out about the black schools in the townships, and especially in Atteridgeville. What Mr Moseneke told me was a sad tale. I was shocked. He started telling me about the collapse of black education.

Firstly, he mentioned that under the National Party's rule, an amount of say R10, would be spent on the education of a white pupil. Only R5 would be spent on the education of a child of Indian origin. Only R2 for the education of a coloured child, someone from mixed parentage. And most importantly, the education of a black child received just R1. The ratio of spending on whites was 10:1, compared to black pupils. This was why pupils at white schools that had electricity could learn about computers and have overhead projectors. But not for blacks.

White schools had sporting facilities. For blacks, there were none.

When it came to teachers, most white teachers obtained a university degree after finishing their Grade 12 year at school; and a fourth-year diploma, known as the Higher Education Diploma.

Most black teachers were far less qualified. They had a pass from a lower level of high school—the equivalent of a Grade 10, which was followed by only one year of further education after leaving school. More worrying was that these black teachers were paid a miserable salary, earning around a tenth of what white teachers did.

An even more frightening disclosure was the overcrowding facing townships schools. Although the development of more schools and premises had been planned and the buildings were laid out in a concept stage, a halt had been decreed by the government. The government's solution was to introduce what was called the platoon system. If the school daily programme started at 7.30am, the headmaster and teachers would teach until 1.00pm. They would all then vacate the school premises and buildings immediately to be replaced by another completely new headmaster, teacher body and group of pupils. The afternoon group would start their teaching at 1.00pm staying until 6.30pm in the evening.

Because of classroom shortages, the younger pupils started their lessons in the classrooms when it was too cold for them. The older students started their early morning classes outside under trees or some other shelter. As the school day got warmer, the younger children would swap, and have their lessons under trees; rotating with the older children whose teachers had the chalkboard, and other teaching amenities.

The afternoon school, or platoon, reversed the timetable to ensure that the younger and more vulnerable children could be taught in the warmer hours under the trees, and have access to the school buildings and classrooms when the temperature started dropping.

Mr Moseneke listed all the schools scheduled for Atteridgeville, which were unfortunately only in the planning or concept stages. So much needed to be done.

At this stage, the government went a step further in their grand and wicked design to oppress black people. In early 1976, they mandated that blacks would no longer be taught in the English language. In future, blacks would be taught lessons in schools with the Afrikaans language forming a dual medium of instruction. The student body was livid. The youth had sometimes accused their parents of not doing more to object to the repressive system. Sadly, they accused their parents of being sell-outs; for lying down instead of standing up against the injustice.

That all changed. On 16 June 1976, the schoolchildren of Soweto rose up in anger—anger against the education system, which had been lowered further by the introduction of Afrikaans as the dual medium of instruction. The police could not quell the riots. People died. Children died. Others were injured. There was rioting in Soweto. The uprising spread across the country like wildfire. Even students from universities and technikons joined forces.

There is a museum in Soweto named the Hector Pieterson Museum. Hector lost his life during the riots, and the harrowing image of the fatally shot 12-year-old being carried in the arms of the young Mbuyisa Makhubu while his sister Antoinette ran alongside them was seen around the world. The picture was taken by Sam Nzima, a reporter on *The Sowetan*, a well-known local newspaper.

Business had been moving along comfortably for our firm and the staff members. One such staff member was a filing clerk named Charles Mathibe. A good man. A conscientious worker.

Suddenly, Charles burst into my office. "Come, come! Urgent—very urgent! Djundju is in big trouble!"

Djundju was Charles' son. He was in his final year of school near Witsieshoek, near the Lesotho border. His parents thought that this smaller school might bolster his chances of receiving a better education in later years.

We jumped into my car and sped down Proes Street to the far west end. The Pass Office was there. That was where all blacks had to be registered under the pass laws. But there was a small jail or cell nearby for pass law infringers. No windows. Only a small vent or opening for air, just below the roof, near the gutter. Charles and I went to the back, unobserved by the policeman. We could hear Djundju and speak into the opening, and he could hear us too.

He whispered that he had been caught and charged with treason. We all knew that a conviction of treason carried the death sentence. Or jail, but with no suspended sentence. The minimum jail sentence carried a mandatory sentence of five years, nothing less and usually far more. Examples of this included Dikgang Moseneke, who was imprisoned for 10 years and later, would become a revered Deputy Chief Justice; and of course, Nelson Mandela, for life.

It was 17 June 1976, the day after the student riots in Soweto. That evening, Djundju and a friend, Ivan Lengoasa, had decided to build a bonfire to burn books outside the schoolrooms on a concrete walkway under the overhanging tin roof. They did this as a show of allegiance with the protesting Soweto students. He claimed it was only a small fire. His school was at Witsieshoek in the Eastern Free State. The police acted immediately, raiding the school, locking them up and charging them with treason.

Then his sisters, Joyce and Yaya, arrived. They were in tears and were frightened that Charles, their father, would lose his job at the law firm. That would have been catastrophic. Charles implored me not to say a word to the office. Keep quiet. I, too, felt very afraid. I resolved not to tell the law firm partners. All of us were petrified.

I went inside and spoke briefly to the white Special Branch policeman. He confirmed the charge of treason, and that the case would probably be heard near the school where the offence occurred.

Yaya had married Dups Isaiah Matsaneng. He worked at Sun City. Waiting for Djundju's trial they had a baby, a little boy. In keeping with tradition, they had to choose a name. They named him Donald Lindsay Matsaneng (after me!).

Having been charged in the Orange Free State, the trial took place at the District Court in Welkom. I briefed Vernon Neumann. He argued that this was a small fire; no danger to property or life. No damage. We got thumped. The judge felt some sympathy for the accused but he knew that his hands were tied. Conviction. Five years. No Appeal. Robben Island. There, Djundju was to meet so many struggle stalwarts. People like Nelson Mandela, Walter Sisulu, Dikgang Moseneke, and many others.

All that time, we didn't say anything to the law firm.

Donald Lindsay later died in a car accident. He had been studying mechanical engineering at the University of Pretoria. I was amazed at the level of speeches from his young university friends at his funeral—so much beautiful poetry!

After leaving the Robben Island prison, Djundju came and worked with us at the Get Ahead Foundation.

The turmoil at the schools and universities galvanised many members of the business world to do something. Led by top businessmen Harry Oppenheimer and Anton Rupert, the Urban Foundation was formed. They undertook to start addressing many of the problems created by the apartheid system. The leaders asked Judge Steyn from the Cape Court to leave the bench so he could become the CEO of the Urban Foundation. He went on to pilot many reforms and was a very hard worker, and was followed by Sam van Coller, who also played a determining role.

My most memorable interaction with the Urban Foundation was with Brian Whitaker. He and I tackled the appalling school system, especially in Atteridgeville. I was able to give Brian the notes I had complied with rough sketch plans I had after that good meeting with Mr SJS Moseneke. I hoped that we were able to pave the way for the building of much-needed structures.

6 ~ USA

Early on, we realised that we were on a hiding to nothing as far as cash flows were concerned. Our initial backers of the original company, Get Ahead Limited, had said their pleasant goodbyes. This is where Bishop Tutu stepped into the breach. He offered to join our board of this new not-for-profit NGO, Get Ahead Foundation. He was a big drawcard. Others who were on the board at different times, apart from the chairman, Dr Motlana, included Snowy Mashigo, Thabo Lesolang, Israel Skosana, Daphne Motsepe, Sizwe Tati, Percy Nkuna, Mpumzi Pupuma, and Dikgang Moseneke. Desmond Tutu hadn't yet called for sanctions and disinvestment—that came later, but he did kindly introduce me to the Reverend Leon Sullivan from the USA.

US companies doing business in South Africa were very much in the limelight. They were starting to be questioned as to why they were doing business in South Africa. Eventually, this led to the formulation of what became known as the Sullivan Principles. These principles formed part of a code expounded by Reverend Leon Sullivan, who had become a rather vocal critic of the South African government. He was constantly lobbying the US government and corporations to become proactive in their condemnation of South Africa and to match their words with deeds—the deeds of disinvesting from or imposing sanctions on South Africa. He ultimately succeeded in persuading the Department of State to agree to adopt his code to be observed by US companies doing business in South Africa.

The Sullivan Principles initially set out six different areas, or principles, with the aim of applying pressure on South African companies in protest of apartheid. The Principles evolved over time but sought to promote non-segregation, health, housing, fair employment and black advancement, among other aspects. Simon Steward of Chase Manhattan later proposed a seventh principle to encompass small informal traders, and that was right up the Get Ahead Foundation's alley.

The Sullivan Principles imposed a heavy-duty or obligation on any US company doing business in South Africa. Directives were given to the companies as to what they should do. The companies would then have to perform. Depending on their performance, they were given a rating or a score. This rating was adjudicated by Arthur D. Little, a consultancy from Boston, USA. To score well on the rating system, US companies had to be proactive in addressing all principles.

In particular, their efforts were divided into their corporate spending across these different areas. A percentage of the company's annual turnover had to be directed towards these programmes.

Over and above this, the Sullivan scorecard was made up of 'sweat' effort. Companies, through their employees, had to prove their support towards initiatives in the fields of education, housing, health and black advancement.

The adoption by the US companies in South Africa of the Sullivan Principles meant a radical shift in day-to-day business practice. All of a sudden, the CEO of the company had to become proactive himself. He had to score points for the system by visiting schools, or hospitals, or advising educationists. His time and effort were no longer directed to running the company full-time to achieve profits because he had an additional role to now play.

This new dimension was translated right down through the company. Employees had to become proactively involved in some way or another. Some were directed towards health programmes. Others were aimed at education. Others concerned themselves with lobbying the government organisations to either change the laws; or to interpret and apply them differently when it came to the application of the laws on the treatment of blacks.

At the end of each year, companies had to complete a scoresheet showing their expenditure on corporate social responsibility programmes—but particularly those in the seven areas as defined by the Sullivan Principles. They then had to detail the manhours spent by their employees in becoming proactively involved in these projects. This involvement could relate to visiting hospitals; clinics; giving advice on health issues; and mentoring small businesses. Personnel from large corporations were now involved in assisting on education issues when they might not necessarily be fully qualified to do so, yet every piece of advice was always warmly received by each recipient. Every hour spent was also charted up on the scoresheet for the end of year reporting.

All this new activity became very onerous. Many of the US companies doing business in South Africa were heard to complain that it was unfair that they had been singled out whereas this did not apply to any of their German, British, or Japanese counterparts. These other foreign-owned companies were seen to be far less involved in corporate social activity and were believed to be devoting more time to running the commercial side of their businesses.

A very important decision was taken by Get Ahead Foundation to set up a company in the USA. This was because it was known that US foundations were keen to assist the disadvantaged in South Africa. Starting in the 1930s, when the Carnegie Foundation conducted very detailed research and produced a report on poverty and the reasons causing poverty, the growing international hostility to South Africa meant that US foundations decided to become more proactive in South Africa.

They became big givers of funds but they too had their rules. They would only give to certain projects where the results and benefits could be clearly seen and measured. The Council of Foundations in the US regularly held seminars on South Africa. South Africans would be invited to speak and outline the difficulties facing blacks in South Africa.

Helpful suggestions were made as to how foundations could cooperate. Mostly, this cooperation was in the form of grant-giving. Some of the major foundations that were proactive in my early stages in Soweto were the Kellogg Foundation, Kaizer Foundation, Hewlett Foundation, Packard Foundation, Ford Foundation—to name a few. There were many others, and we were very grateful for their support.

To set up a company in the USA we needed to make sure that once registered, our US company would be given the necessary tax exemption. This meant that any funds given to the US company, once registered, would be tax-efficient for the donor, in terms of Section 501(c)(3) of the US tax laws. There were tax breaks for a person or corporation giving money to a registered 501(c)(3) charitable organisation.

This highly sought-after status given by the Internal Revenue Services was a necessity for South African charity organisations. Without this tax exemption, it was pointless going on a fundraising drive or mission in the US. While foundations and corporations may have been kind in listening to appeals from the needy in South Africa, donors' hands were tied in that they needed to ensure that the grantee had the necessary tax exemption certificate.

This presented a big obstacle to us. How could we, sitting in Soweto, hope to set up a 501(c)(3) tax-exempt body in the US?

Corinne and John Roy live in Johannesburg. John had been a top-ranked squash player. He had been invited to join the Jesters Club. The Jesters play a hard game of squash. They are very competent players. They organise different matches against other clubs and around the country. Occasionally, they tour overseas. John had been on a Jester's tour to the USA and there, he met and played squash against John Graves.

John Graves' son, Peter, decided to visit Gabon in West Africa. John called John and Corinne Roy in Johannesburg and asked if Peter could come to South Africa and stay with them. They willingly agreed. They suggested he meet me in Soweto. We did, and Peter offered immediately to help set up the Get Ahead Foundation in the US with 501(c)(3) status.

Armed with a letter from Bishop Tutu, Peter was a firebrand—he started attracting people to serve on our board in the US.

People who joined immediately were Walter Carrington, a big NAACP member, as was Derek Humphries. Senator Edward Kennedy was agreeable, as were David Miller, Daniel Rose, Joe MacMahon, Bill Hayden and Maurice Tempelsman, who was also the consort of the late Jackie Kennedy Onassis until her death in 1994.

From them, I learned about the dictum to be a board member: Give, or get out. Stern stuff!

To accommodate Senator Kennedy, we accepted his kind offer to have our board meetings at his office in Russell Hall.

7 ~ Sanctions & Disinvestment

In the mid-1980s, Bishop Tutu shifted gears. He publicly called on the government to take steps to abandon apartheid and its laws, regulations and practices. He invited them to react within a month and prove their stated intentions in achieving that aim.

He waited a month. There was no response from the government. So, he again called on them to take steps, giving them another month.

At the end of that second month, the Bishop called a press conference addressing South Africans, but also the wider international audience; foreign governments, embassies, companies, NGOs, human rights organisations, and the international press—it had very wide coverage.

He spoke quietly, unwaveringly, and with energy and purpose. He explained how apartheid laws were impacting black people. They were not citizens in their own country. They had no rights. He recounted how he had called on the South African government to dismantle the oppressive system, to no avail.

He called on the wider international community to impose sanctions on South Africa, and to start the process of disinvesting their companies and investments from South Africa. The ripple effect was enormous. I recall the first reaction came from Willard Butcher, the CEO of Chase Manhattan in New York. He said that Chase was closing up in South Africa shop immediately. Other companies followed. Where international companies had infrastructure on the ground—factories, plants, machinery—South African companies clamoured to buy these exiting companies at fire-sale prices, often having a buy-back clause if the situation were to change back later.

The effects of the call for sanctions were far-reaching and extensive. No longer were most white South Africans happy with the loveable Bishop. On the contrary, the majority of the white population started disliking him immensely.

"How could he call for sanctions against our lovely country?! Can you imagine the effect it will have on our economy? Just think of the loss of jobs, alone?" People were very outspoken about him.

The call for sanctions had its own effect on our little company, Get Ahead. Some of the sponsoring companies quietly walked away, not renewing their pledges for future funding. Others were more forthright, asking, "How can we support your company when your own board member calls for sanctions against our company?"

A cogent example happened at a public meeting held at the then upmarket Carlton Hotel in Johannesburg. It was at one such meeting arranged by the American Chamber of Commerce (AMCHAM) when Jack Clarke, the CEO of IBM in Armonk, New York, was the guest speaker. He broke away from his pre-prepared speech, took off his spectacles and said over the microphone, to the 250 people there: "Now, I want to address a special plea to Mr MacRobert sitting at the back there. I want him to ask his fellow board member, Bishop Tutu, to stop calling for sanctions against South Africa, and to stop the call that USA companies must divest their holdings from their subsidiary companies in South Africa."

That couldn't be clearer. But the fear gripped me.

It got worse at an even bigger meeting of ASSOCOM, the Association of South African Commerce. The guest speaker on that occasion was Raymond Ackerman, the founder and chairman of a leading publicly listed company on the Johannesburg Stock Exchange. He too broke from his pre-prepared speech, when he said: "I want to call on Mr MacRobert at the back, to implore his fellow board member, Bishop Tutu, to stop his call for sanctions and disinvestment."

Some American companies went as far as telling us to never visit them again. I was once asked to leave the office of Colgate at 300 Park Avenue, New York. Some other companies were the same, like Reader's Digest. Jenny Williams, our fundraiser, also had a tough time. She fielded many blows and knocks aimed at us and our board members.

St Francis, our Anglican church in Waterkloof, Pretoria, took the bold step to invite Bishop Tutu to address the congregation on his reasoning. As you can imagine, it was a full house; people standing at the back, sitting in the aisles, the choir stalls brimming with people trying to get seats. All wanted to hear the Bish speak. And to voice their opposition.

He started speaking quietly and said he appreciated what sanctions and disinvestment could do to the economy of the country—it could result in job losses, especially from the workforce, his people, black people. He explained how apartheid laws were so repressive that they impacted the lives of everybody, but mainly black people. After detailing the compendium of laws, he wanted to address us on family law, and he did so because we in the congregation have families.

"Let me just tell you one family story," said Bishop Tutu. "It is about a man who lives in the country, far from any town or established village. He has no work. He cannot feed his family. So, he agrees with his wife that he should go to the city, to seek employment. Once in the city, he goes first to the pass office to get himself registered. He has 72 hours to find a job. For accommodation, he goes to the men's hostel, finds a concrete bed. He is lucky and gets a job. He starts sending a little of his pay packet back to his wife and two small children. He does so on a regular basis. Small amounts each month. He keeps up his monthly support his family. At the end of his first 11 months, he is obligated by law, to return home for a month. The pass laws only allow him to stay as a migrant worker for 11 months. Thereafter, he has to take leave for a month. When he returns, he must get his pass book stamped; find accommodation, and hopefully his same job as before.

He resumes monthly payments to his wife. But then he skips a month, and does the same again, two months later. The money at home starts drying up. Because why? He has taken in another woman—somebody from town. Maybe a bit better educated. And so, the new lady starts putting pressure on the man to pay for her as well. He cannot afford to pay for two wives and a second family. So, he does the obvious, and pays each woman during alternating months.

The original wife becomes distraught. The situation at home is very bad. She decides to catch a train to the city to find her husband. She has to carry the smaller child on her hip. She becomes exhausted. She has never seen a traffic light before, a light that switches from green to red. Some kindly soul guides her across the pedestrian crossing. With all the anxiety and stress, sadly, she becomes mentally deranged and is hospitalised. The family disintegrates. Nothing is left."

Tutu paused for a moment before asking the audience: "Do you want that to happen to you and your family?"

Silence.

Then big applause. His markers hit home, and his message was understood.

It wasn't only businesses who were mad at Desmond Tutu. Most whites of any political persuasion were in the same boat, however, the tide had already started turning.

8 ~ Politics & Sports

Every five years in South Africa, we would have a general election, when voters would vote for one of the three parties: the Nationalists or ruling National Party; the opposition party, the United Party; followed by the tiny Progressive Party led by its one elected member, the indomitable and incredibly feisty Helen Suzman. On election day, voters would go to their polling stations where the political parties had erected tents near the polling booths. These tents served to provide information about each party and how to cast one's vote but also to ensure the particulars of voters were correctly captured.

Being in the majority by far, the Nationalists' tent was the biggest. Quite a lot smaller was the tent for the opposition, the United Party. Then came the littlest of them all, the Progressive Party's tent. Manned by only five or six ladies who were all volunteer workers, I remember that small tent tucked away in a corner at the Waterkloof polling station. Its sides were rolled up so you could look outside to see people coming, and passers-by could look into the tent to see the volunteers working diligently to check voter lists—except the Progressive Party got so few voters, it was almost laughable. I marvelled at friends like Blanche van Schaik, Anne Macdonald and Ann Job, who sat there so loyally. People could walk into their chosen party's tent and would almost gape at these ladies who were all there was to see. They were fabulous!

The way the Progressive Party tent was set up also meant Blanche and her colleagues could see out and check who had gone into the other parties' tents. It was amazing for us that so many of the people we knew were streaming into the other tents. We were surprised that our friends, all from our same neighbourhood and all English speakers, had flocked to the other tents, especially the big tent of the National Party. This was originally mainly an Afrikaans-speaking stronghold, but now vastly swelled by the English-speaking group.

As I stood there, I told Ann, Anne and Blanche about some of my canvassing experiences for the Progressive Party. Often, people would politely decline and say, "no thank you". Others were more aggressive. On one occasion, a man slammed the door in my face.

During one of my rounds in our neighbourhood, I was dropping in to ask residents if they would kindly donate money to our Progressive Party, a big catch presented itself—a big businessman with a big house and two big luxury cars to complete it all. To my astonishment, he said that he and his wife admired Helen Suzman, but he could not be seen to give any money to her, or the Progressive Party. Also, money given cannot be traced from his bank account, so he asked me to come past his front gate at 6.00pm on Sunday night, when all was quiet, almost dark. He said he would leave money, cash, in a brown paper bag in his letterbox, which he would leave slightly open. I collected the brown bag. That was the state of mind of the electorate. Driven by fear.

The Progressive Party needed to hold a regional annual general meeting to receive reports, and particularly, to elect office bearers for the next year. The meeting was scheduled to take place at the Union Hotel, in Pretoria. Owned by Helen Suzman's family trust, it was a comfortable setting. Our region consisted of the whole of the Northern Transvaal, stretching from Johannesburg, all the way up to the border with Zimbabwe—a huge area. I felt quite important because I was elected as vice chairman for that big area, and to cap it all, I was also elected to be chairman of the fundraising committee. Quite a big job. The irony was, although I had been duly elected, only five people showed up for that regional meeting. I clearly remember Daryll and Frances Moss, along with another couple, Chris and Dirkie Gilfillan. The paucity of numbers flowed from the overbearing pressure created by the political environment at the time. The Afrikaans press spoke openly about the *swart gevaar*, or black peril, often with a danger warning sign to 'alert' people to beware the rising black tide.

We were delighted when, in 1974, the Progressive Party won a further six seats in Parliament to lift the sole Helen Suzman representative tally to a total of seven members. Still less than 5% of the 220 MPs yet, we felt the tide was indeed turning. The voices of blacks now stood a chance of being heard, even on a limited scale. Or so we thought.

Buoyed by this upward movement, I proposed to the region and its council of five members that we organise a black-tie dinner at the Union Hotel. I said we must invite Gordon Waddell, one of the seven new members in Parliament, to be the main speaker, along with Tony Bloom who had performed so well in Johannesburg as Gordon's election agent. As the chairman of Premier Milling, one of the original sponsors of Get Ahead Limited, Tony immediately agreed to speak. I started calling on the members of the Progressive Party who lived in Pretoria, and friends who I thought would be keen to listen in on the proceedings. I invited them to attend the event. Sadly, many people politely declined. Some said that Pretoria, as the capital of the country and seat of the government of the National Party, was light years behind Johannesburg, the business centre. With only eight confirmed attendees, we had to cancel the engagement.

Later on, after having worked in Soweto for about four years, I realised that the Progressive Party, which I had dutifully and faithfully served since 1959, would not be the right vehicle to address the aspirations of black people. So, in 1987, I wrote to Tony Bloom offering my resignation from the party, now called the Progressive Reform Party following its merger with the Reform Party in 1975. He wrote a very kind letter of thanks and bid me well in my future endeavours.

While my political aspirations may have come to an end, I couldn't help but notice how politics and sports are so closely and inextricably linked.

When I started working in Soweto, I met up with Geoff Mphakati, the kind soul who, as children, had taught me that wonderful Xhosa hymn that is now part of our national anthem. Geoff started his own print shop in Mamelodi outside Pretoria. He was a hard worker who always delivered his goods on time. One day I asked whether he was still playing golf. "Yes," he replied, but in Johannesburg at a golf course where blacks were welcomed. The Group Areas Act was overlooked by some benign white golfers. So, I asked if he would agree to me nominating him to become a playing member at my country club, the Pretoria Country Club. Geoff agreed but I needed a seconder to support his application. I turned to a good friend, Francois Junod, a senior lawyer. He willingly signed the forms. We went to the designated meeting with the captain of golf. He drew our attention to the club rules that stated membership was only open to all people who were registered as voters. That meant only whites. We were beaten by the Nationalist machine.

Geoff carried on playing at the friendly courses in Johannesburg and sadly passed away when I was travelling overseas in 2004. Jenny Williams and Pam Taylor from Get Ahead said his funeral was a splendid occasion, with Geoff's family hiring the National State Theatre in Pretoria.

In the 1980s, I became an active member of an organisation called Round Table Southern Africa. Its membership was open to young men under the age of 40. When you turned 40 years old, you automatically left or resigned. Round Table did a lot of project work to help the needy; the poor, elderly and sick. Realising that things were changing in South Africa, the Round Table movement started a parallel organisation, called Sable, the first letter 'S' being a play on the first letter of 'Table' from the name from 'Round Table'. It was a good attempt to overcome some of the racial divisions in the country. I met up with people from Sable, like Maxwell Salsone and Vicky Christian, who would later become a highly qualified accountant. But I felt we should go a bit further. We should not have a parallel organisation for people of colour. So, through quiet lobbying and discussion, in 1987, I proposed that my friend Mala Carrim should join our white Round Table, from Pretoria. That proposal went through all the channels without any unnecessary fuss. I was grateful to members from then Pietersburg, Rusty Gillett and Jan van Zyl, along with John Maynard and Deleeuw Swart from Pretoria, for their support.

Vicky and I got up to some tricks. South Africans love the sport of rugby with a huge passion. It is an understatement to describe the frenzy and fervour for the game. We have prided ourselves as being one of the top rugby countries in the world and two years ago, in 2019, we became world champions for the third time. Our national team, the famous Springboks, were led forcefully by a stunning rugby player, Siya Kolisi—our first ever black captain.

I was impressed before the World Cup when the national team's coach, Rassie Erasmus, openly said that South Africa has so many good black players coming into the system that there was no problem recruiting players for the Springboks against a quota, or racial demographic system. Once the war cry for Black Lives Matter went viral, the Springboks' coach and team easily sailed over the bar compared to other sport disciplines.

When Vicky and I got chatting one evening, long ago, and way before the 2020 World Rugby event, I discovered that not only was he a passionate rugby follower but had played very good rugby at an advanced level. Of course, that was at a time when only whites played the game at a national level, and others like Vicky played in the 'other' leagues for blacks and coloureds. Vicky, being classified as coloured, did not play with whites. But I asked him if he had ever watched the national rugby team, the Springboks, play an international test match at Loftus, the holy ground for rugby in Pretoria. It would be the equivalent of watching a game at Twickenham in England. He hadn't. So, I asked him if he would like to watch a test at Loftus. "Absolutely!" came the emphatic reply. We both knew that if we were caught, big trouble would follow—for both of us! I went ahead and booked two seats on the side opposite the grandstand where the rowdy, and rough guys get their seats. I even bought us two deer stalking caps to firstly, shade our eyes against the sun, but more importantly, to cover our heads. Vicky had described his hair as being a bit woolly, or spindly and said it would be a dead giveaway.

We got there early and bought a small bag of citrus fruit because the players on our side of the stadium love to throw things at the referee when he makes an incorrect decision. Also, we bought scarves to hang around our necks, one having the green and gold colours with the flying springbok emblem; the other being a blue scarf depicting a rampant, snorting bull and the emblem of the Loftus home team, the Blue Bulls. Wow! We were set to go.

The game was a resounding success. Firstly, the Springboks won! Secondly, Vicky joined in the throwing of objects at the referee. Thirdly, he and I got hoarse shouting for our team. That passion and the temperature on the ground got much hotter than in the streets outside. It was a great day!

But the Springboks followers needed a lot of time to mull over the game, to recount the big moments of the game, and to make absolutely clear that the game was won by a mile-and-a-half. All the locals would get together at the nearby Harlequin Rugby Club to confirm their fantastic knowledge of the game of rugby, where Vicky and I would also go. I bought us our first beer. Then Vicky bought the second round. And of course, I slowly introduced Vicky to good friends. Big Dan was the president of the club. Others included Jacot, Rusty, Brian, Woody, Klinkie, Smithy, Tiny and his brother-in-law, Mike, Klippie—all with lovely South African flavoured names. We had such fun, and Vicky bought his fair share of beers, buying a round for everyone.

Getting to closing time, Klippie asked Vicky: "Haven't we met before?"

"Yes," replied Vicky. "At a Sable function—where blacks and coloureds only meet."

"Whew!" said Klippie. "You could have fooled me. In fact, you did. All of us whiteys!"

"Great!" exclaimed Big Dan. "You bought liquor here at our bar, for us all, but illegally. That was against the law. Fantastic—I have been wanting to do that for some time!"

"Shit!" said Woody to me. "Don, you brought Vicky into Loftus, the den of rugby. Can you imagine if the Ku Klux Klan, all 55 000 of them, stormed into the stadium, what they would have done to you?"

We ran.

9 ~ Education

During apartheid, black children had to go to black schools. White children had to go to white schools. The government spent a tenth of the amount educating a black child, compared to a white child. Black schools did not always have electricity, and many of them were terribly overcrowded with up to 70 pupils in a classroom with one teacher. There were no overhead projectors. Computers were just starting to arrive in the white schools and were definitely not part of the inventory of black schools.

Also, white schools had lovely libraries with books. Research could be conducted in a quiet atmosphere. Most black schools did not have a library with books at all.

My uncle Mello who was almost like a second father to me—encouraged me to go into intellectual property law practice. He was key in the founding of St Alban's College, a private school in Pretoria. He sadly died at a young age in 1980. At his wake, which was at our house, some of the more senior members of St Alban's College governing board approached me and asked whether I would like to join them on the board. Their idea was marketed very cleverly and was with a view to taking the place of Mello as chairman. I readily accepted because St Alban's was starting to get a good reputation. My two older sons, Bruce and Guy, had just started there.

Monty Knoll took over from Mello as acting chairman of the executive committee of the governing board. After about a year, he and the elder board members said it would be a good idea to now have a formal election for the new chairman. The rest of us on the governing board thought that this was a good idea. However, it was proposed that we should send our nominations in writing to Monty at his particular postal address. This would be in the form of a secret postal ballot. We all agreed.

To my utter surprise, at the next council meeting, they had elected me, the youngest member of the council, to be chairman. They had engineered this. This was a bit of collusion. The voting went 13 to 1, which showed that I was the sole voter against the other 13 voters, or members. I now had to take over as chairman of the executive committee of a recently-opened school that was growing—both in reputation and pupil numbers. With it came many problems and issues such as the building of new classrooms; the erection of more boarding houses; establishing whether the swimming pool was long enough or not, and so on.

Around the early 1980s, some of the white private schools were becoming anxious about doing something and felt they should start admitting black children. This was being spoken about but very little, or nothing was actually done.

Then the school chaplain, Reverend David Swanepoel, spoke to me very firmly one day. He said that St Alban's College was a church school. This meant that we were supposed to practice church ideals. Could the church school stand by idly and not address the adverse situation in black education? "What do you propose to do about apartheid?" he asked me. He threw down a challenge. After much thought and consultation with other governing board members, I made two very tentative proposals, underscoring that they were tentative.

The first was that we should be prepared to break the law and start admitting black children as pupils to the school. This was an act of defiance, in a way. We debated the matter long and hard. However, we felt that it was our duty, as members of the church, to take this step. A sad day was the resignation from the council of a good man, Judge Frank Kirk-Cohen. He explained that he was fully in favour of the proposal, but as a Judge of the High Court, he could not break the law.

A resolution was taken that we would now start seeking out potential students who would not be too stressed with the academic curriculum. This would be a difficult task because we were fully aware of the fact that the education of black schoolchildren then was inferior to the education received by white children. Yet, despite these drawbacks, some of the black schools were producing some very talented children. We needed to find them.

Fortunately, the church was able to help us in the black townships. The church membership was strong there. They knew of some bright young children and so we were able to start selecting our first pupils.

But the Catholic schools were first.

On 1 January 1981, a number of Catholic schools throughout the country opened their doors and admitted not one or two black pupils as we had contemplated; rather, they admitted 10 to 15 new pupils at several schools in the city and the country. The government was outraged. They ranted and raved at the Catholics. There were public pronouncements from the Prime Minister. The Minister of Education said that this was all illegal and threatened the schools with closure. They firmly held their ground. To their credit, none of the Catholic church schools were ever closed down and they produced hundreds of well-educated pupils.

The Anglicans were just behind the Catholics and St Alban's College admitted its first two black pupils in 1982. We were the first Anglican church school in the country to admit pupils of colour. And in all the years we did this, surprisingly there was never any real threat of closure or opposition from the government. Somehow, the Department of Education, while not comfortable with what was going on, did not take any proactive steps to shut the school down or chase away these new pupils.

There have been some wonderful success stories of pupils from disadvantaged backgrounds who have attended these private schools. One such person was Vusi Radebe. He lived in the township known as Alexandra, just to the north of Johannesburg. He had been a caddy at the Wanderers Golf Course—all his friends were caddies there. He was offered the chance to go to St Alban's College on a bursary. He studied there and completed further studies at tertiary education institutions.

He is now the deputy CEO of a company that has just listed on the stock exchange. He has made his mark in the professional world—from being a caddy at the golf course at the Wanderers, he is now a member at the Wanderers Golf Course and plays off a six handicap.

There are many others like him who came through this quite 'illegal' system, but St Alban's College made its mark in another area.

Still being admonished by Reverend Swanepoel, I was mindful of the fact that white schools had tremendous facilities. They had libraries and projectors, and some were starting to develop computer centres. But the black schools had none of these facilities.

I suggested to the governing board that I examine the possibility of opening our facilities to students from disadvantaged areas in the afternoons and evenings when these facilities would not be used by our day pupils. The board was wonderful. They gave me blanket authority to start moving forward and to make investigations.

I realised that no project would be successful unless we consulted with people from the townships. We would have to get their approval. We could not come in with another white programme and say "this is good for you". Blacks were tired of that. There had to be a consultative process. Through contacts in Atteridgeville township towards the west of Pretoria, I was fortunate to meet up again with the highly-respected Mr SJS Moseneke.

I explained that St Alban's College had excellent facilities. I asked, if I was able to find the money, could he endorse the idea of teachers from Atteridgeville coming to St Alban's in the afternoons and evenings to be upskilled and upgraded. Mr Moseneke was ecstatic!

He agreed that this was clearly needed. He gave the illustration of how teachers from black townships would be trying to teach English when this was not their first but rather, their second language. Teachers would be trying to teach this to children who, similarly, did not have English as a first language. This meant that teachers fell foul of the English language and grammar, and often a teacher would say, as an example given by Mr Moseneke, "Sophie, she is a girl", instead of "Sophie is a girl". The incorrect insertion of the word "she" in the English sentence was as a result of a direct translation from an African language such as Sesotho.

And so, with Mr Moseneke's support, I then went to Mamelodi, in the east of Pretoria. There, I met a Mr Mokgabo. A respected educationist, he had been a teacher and was also now an inspector of schools. He too was supportive.

This was the start. Separate meetings were held during which we explained what we were aiming to do: give the teachers from Atteridgeville and Mamelodi lessons so that they could improve their qualifications. Hopefully, this would also improve their teaching skills.

There was an overwhelming vote of support. This was surprising, until we learnt some of the reasons.

It turned out that most teachers at the black schools in the townships had only passed grade 10 followed by a one-year diploma course. Most white teachers had at least passed grade 12 and obtained a three-year bachelor's degree from a university, with a fourth year to get a Higher Education Diploma. Therefore, white teachers were far better qualified than their black counterparts.

But it went further. The government paid teachers according to their qualifications. While it was acceptable in black schools for a teacher to have only a grade 10 qualification with a one-year diploma, this was certainly not going to be the case in the white schools. The salaries were far lower for a black teacher.

The teachers were overjoyed at the prospect of being able to study further to obtain their matric, or the equivalent of a grade 12. They endorsed our proposals wholeheartedly. Admittedly, it took us a bit of time to realise why we had met with such overwhelming support. On the other hand, we saw this as a good opportunity to not only upskill teachers from the townships, but also to use the opportunity to give them upskilling in teaching methodology. This was also appreciated by the teachers.

And so, Outreach was born. This name, Outreach, was one which I coined as it carried the connotation of reaching out into the community. The *Financial Mail* in South Africa recorded in 1982 that we were the first school in South Africa to start an 'outreach' programme for blacks.

We started in a small way but held meetings both at St Alban's College and in the townships of Mamelodi and Atteridgeville. We explained what we were trying to do. The teachers had given us their support. We then invited potential sponsors. We needed to raise money to cover heavy transport costs, to be able to ferry the teachers from Mamelodi or Atteridgeville to St Alban's. We also had to pay the instructors who were giving up their free time. We were asking these instructors, who were normal teachers at St Alban's, to give these Outreach lessons when they were supposed to be off duty.

Jenny Williams stepped up to the plate. A born fundraiser, she and I held meetings with potential sponsors, and were delighted when the Dutch government became the first foreign government to lend its support. They were very generous in recognising the need to upskill the teachers from the black townships, and were soon followed by some of the larger companies such as Johnson & Johnson, whose head office was in New Brunswick, New Jersey, USA. Here, Roger Crawford, who was later to become President of the American Chamber of Commerce, was a leading light. He certainly helped motivate other American companies to give support. We were most grateful for that.

The instructors were superb. They were ably led by John Bojé, an experienced teacher. He motivated his fellow teachers at St Alban's to become instructors at the evening Outreach classes.

We initially picked up a fair amount of resistance from the parent body at St Alban's College. Some of them said that they were already paying fees to this private school. These fees were to pay for the teachers' salaries. Why should the teachers then take on additional duties which might seriously impact their regular everyday teaching activities? We had to go to great lengths to explain that the instructors, who were normal teachers by day at the St Alban's School, were giving these lessons to the black teachers in their spare time. We also had to explain that to motivate these instructors, they had to be paid. This resistance was typical of the white attitude of the day.

After a while, everyone calmed down and the parent body accepted that this would not impair the duties of the teachers whose daytime salaries were being paid.

However, Outreach's programme did not quite meet the approval of the authorities. The fact was that we were now expanding our operations to include students of colour at a time when the government had just declared a state of emergency. Talk of education being delivered under the barrel of the gun was of concern.

Whenever inspectors came from the Department of Education to check on the school, which they were entitled by law to, at the top of their list of questions was how many students from the black townships would be coming to the evening classes. What subjects would they be taught? Had we registered these additional pupils as scholars under the education system? And under which system were they registered and being taught—the black or the white system?

We were never given the official go-ahead and the Department of Education never gave us any encouragement. We explained that some of our best stories were of people who had started off with low qualifications were now moving up the education ladder. They were better qualified. They could teach better. More especially, the ripple effect would be felt by those they taught.

This was a considerable advantage to the schools in the black townships.

The programmes expanded and other pupils were taken in for these evening Outreach classes. These pupils were often adults who had lower grades and who wanted to advance themselves. One of the best illustrations was that of Johanna Mahlangu. She was employed by St Alban's College as a cleaner. She had achieved grade 10 at school but the only employment she could find was as a washerwoman in the school laundry.

She enrolled for our night-time Outreach classes. She gained her matric and then was able to secure funding to enable her to study at university. She obtained a bachelor's degree and became a teacher. Hers was one of the many excellent stories of the Outreach initiatives.

Outreach's programmes began to expand. Not only did we aim this at the teachers but decided to focus on school pupils as well. With funding that Jenny organised from the likes of De Beers, Anglo American and many other American companies, we started a programme aimed at upskilling schoolchildren in mathematics and English. We were told by commerce and industry that their reasons for supporting this programme were because the commercial world needed trained people. To get the training, it was essential for potential applicants to have attended a university and obtained tertiary education qualifications. To get there, a pupil must have achieved a matric, but more particularly needed to have good grades in maths and English.

And so, a school upgrading programme called Retsweletse was initiated. Township schools were invited to select their top pupils for this advanced training in maths and English. Retsweletse was hugely popular and successful, with some of the students doing exceptionally well in later years. They were able to gain entrance into a university and obtain degrees that enabled them to get good employment.

I learnt about the power of a candle in the black townships of Soweto and Mamelodi, situated just outside Pretoria.

Up until 1985, Soweto had no electrification. Neither did Mamelodi, and many other townships. This meant that every home could not have a television set, or an electric heater for when it was cold, or an electric kettle or stove.

Soweto was the largest township in Southern Africa, with the highest population by far but it was not a normal city that would have been laid out by town planners with shopping centres, parks, cinemas, sporting grounds and social amenities. It was a sleeping town, a dormitory.

When I visited families in the mid-1980s, I often asked them to show me how they lived at night. A township home was tidy by day with the furniture neatly arranged. But when six or seven people came to sleep there at night, all that changed. Each person had a particular spot on the floor of the lounge. And you could only put your head down on your spot once everybody else had vacated the lounge. This meant that one had to wait for their parents to go to bed in their bedroom before the rest of the family could prepare to go to sleep.

If you were a student at school or at university, living conditions became even more problematic. You could only study when you were not getting in the way of the rest of the family.

This might mean that you had to wait until everybody else had gone to bed or when everyone was lying down on the floor in their allocated spots. Only then could you get into a corner and start your studies.

And in Soweto it was tougher because there was no electrification until the mid-1980s. This meant that people had to study by candlelight. This obviously created difficulties and hardships because it was difficult for a person to study by candlelight. I often thought of the medieval times when there was no formal electricity and how scholars and others must have battled to study or write then.

The inconvenience went further. If you were one of the people already trying to go to sleep on the floor and one of your family members wanted to study by candlelight, this light would continue to shine up the room until very late when the exhausted student blew it out.

1986 turned out to be a difficult year. It was 10 years after the Soweto student uprising in June 1976. In the months and weeks in the run-up to 16 June 1986, there were growing talks of more student uprisings. Students were encouraged to join protest marches. There were stay-aways from work. Public transport would be boycotted.

In early June 1986, the government declared a state of national emergency. Under the emergency regulations, the rule of law was suspended in many areas. Police virtually took over control of the black townships. They could arrest people on a mere suspicion. They did not have to bring them to court to be charged. People were held in detention for long periods of time. They were never really brought to court. At one stage it was reported that 20 000 people were being detained by the government under the security laws.

And even in the black townships such as Mamelodi, outside Pretoria, the police took matters into their own hands. They would knock on doors late at night or force them open and demand to see the whole family. Line them up. Then take away a father or a son believed to be a political activist. Sometimes, this might be the last time the family member was seen.

Around this time, my wife Marianne befriended Marjorie Nkomo who lived in Atteridgeville. They worked together on community projects. The Nkomo children were at the same schools as our children, namely St Mary's DSG and St Alban's College.

Dr Abe Nkomo, Marjorie's husband, was a tremendous critic of the government and very outspoken. He was once detained by the police and Marjorie couldn't find out at which police station he was being held so she sought Marianne's help. The two of them left one Saturday morning to try find Abe. They knew that he was last being held at the Pretoria North police station. They arrived and were not dealt with courteously. Rather they were dealt with rudely. It was almost as if Marjorie should not be interfering with the police duties by coming to visit her husband, and Marianne was a real intruder. Why was a white woman getting involved in these black people's affairs?

Some Saturdays, they would see Abe. On others, they would find that he had been transferred to another jail or police station and they would have to find him, wherever he might be.

With Abe in jail, he could not run his medical practice and there was no income from his side for the family. Marjorie struggled to keep up and it was only over the weekend that she was able to visit Abe. All this became too much of a strain for Marjorie, so Marianne very generously invited two of the Nkomo children, Nolitha and Vuyisile, to come and stay with us. They lived with us in Pretoria not far from their schools for eight months. Marianne or I would take them to school in the morning and Marianne would then collect them after school in the afternoon.

Over weekends, they would go back to Marjorie at the family home in Atteridgeville.

It was not a pleasant time to be in the townships. It was certainly not pleasant at all if one of your family members was detained for weeks on end and you did not know his or her whereabouts. Things were very bleak indeed.

Then an interesting development happened. The St Alban's Outreach programme for schoolchildren was in full swing. The pupils would come in the late afternoon, attend their classes in maths and science and then return home. They explained that with the state of emergency in full swing, all black schools had been shut down in the townships. This meant that the normal school day did not exist. Pupils could not learn. Neither the teachers nor the pupils were going to school at all.

The matric class from Outreach approached me. They were desperate to complete their matriculation examinations. They absolutely needed those certificates to gain entrance to university, and without this, there could be no academic future for them.

At the time, John Bojé headed up the Outreach programme. He was responsible for timetabling. He would sort out the pupils with which class they would have to attend and who would be teaching them. He responded very firmly and warmly to the Outreach pupils' request. He would definitely want to try and help them get their matric certificates. He undertook to ensure that the pupils would receive their education. He went even further and proposed to the school management that the 20 Outreach pupils from Mamelodi township move onto the St Alban's campus for the remainder of their studies—almost four months. They could be housed in the sanatorium. Special beds and sleeping arrangements could be made for them. Management agreed. One by one, the pupils moved quietly from their homes in Mamelodi and came to live on the St Alban's College campus in the white area. But this was clearly against the law.

As the pupils left their homes in Mamelodi, they told their friends that they were going to go and stay with an aunt in the far north. Or with a grandmother in a rural area. Some said that they were going to visit friends in distant places. Out of fear of what the security police might do to the pupils, they did not want their whereabouts to be known. If the bush telegraph let it be known that they had moved into the white area and were staying at the St Alban's College campus, there were dire consequences. They could be arrested by the Special Branch. They were so desperate to make sure they got their instruction that they went to great lengths to fabricate stories as to their whereabouts. Fear played a big part in their lives.

John and the St Alban's staff piled in. Beds were brought into the sanatorium. Extra food was laid on. The children would be well-looked-after as far as their everyday necessities were concerned.

The pupils then went even further. They raised a most interesting request. Now that they were living on St Alban's College campus full-time, could they not be given instruction in all their matriculation subjects, and not only maths and English? They wanted to make absolutely sure that with instruction in all subjects, they would be able to get their matriculation certificates. They needed to get into university. The university degree was the passport to better jobs. With a better job, they could then start supporting their families and start uplifting other members of their family.

It meant a whole lot to not only an individual, but also the extended family of siblings, parents and even grandparents.

The schools in the townships remained closed and police action under the emergency regulations did not permit their opening.

Our newfound pupils at St Alban's discovered that there might be a problem. For the end-of-year matriculation, one had to register at their school. This the pupils had done; they registered through their schools in the townships through the black education system. However, the schools were now closed. The question was raised by our Outreach pupils: "How would they be able to write their exams if their schools were effectively closed?"

I promised to take this up with the Department of Education. I called a senior person. I made a date to see him. I put the children's problem to him. How could the children write their examinations for their matriculation certificates if the schools were still closed? His reply was straightforward: "The schools will be open just in time to enable the children to enter the examination halls of the schools to write their matriculation exams."

In particular, he mentioned that there would be a military presence. Soldiers would guard the halls to ensure the safety of the candidates.

I was not overly impressed with this answer but took it back to St Alban's College and spoke to the Outreach children in the sanatorium. I conveyed the message from the Department of Education about the military guards for examinations.

The response from the children was one of overwhelming shock, alarm and disdain. They rejected the Department of Education's suggestions. They did so for two reasons.

The first was that the schools had been closed since June. It was now September. This meant that the children had not attended any formal school at their township schools for the last three months. The greater concern was how they could prepare for the end of year matriculation examination, due to be written in November. There would be no instruction from their schools. This was why they had asked St Alban's staff to give them instruction in all their matric subjects.

The second reason was even more compelling. The students said that they could not write their matric exams in the township schools under the barrel of a gun. While the security people might protect the children while they were in the examination hall for three or four hours, this was no guarantee of what might happen before the exams or after the exams had been written. The children feared for their own safety.

We now had to develop another strategy—thus began a merry-go-round flurry of activity.

I made an appointment with the senior examiner for the matriculation examinations. I explained the problem. I asked that permission be given to the Mamelodi children for them to be able to register from St Alban's College as it had its own full-time students writing the matric exams. I explained the predicament that the children could not write their matric exams under the barrel of a gun. The senior examiner promised that he would consult with his colleagues at the Department of Education.

He called me after a few days and said that I must put my problem to the Head of the Invigilation Committee. Apparently, there was a separate committee for invigilators who used to ensure good conduct in the examination halls while the pupils were writing their exams.

Generally, this duty fell to the schools whose children were registered for matric purposes. However, there were cases where the invigilation committee had to take the necessary steps to ensure that other outside venues were adequately staffed during the time that the children wrote their exams.

I spoke to the Head of the Invigilation Committee. I asked him how he would feel if his own children were denied the right to sit for their exams. He expressed sympathy and promised to come back to me.

He did so, calling about 10 days later.

He said that while he sympathised with the children, the Invigilation Committee was not the body to make the necessary decision. He said that I should get in touch with the Head of the Venues Committee.

Now we were facing a challenge on time. The exams were to be written in November. We had started this chain of calling, contacting and applying in September. It was now October and time was running out.

I got in touch with the chairman of the Venues Committee. I told him that this was a matter of urgency and asked if I was able to put the case to him. Like the other committee chairmen, he promised that he would also get back to me.

He did so, and fairly soon.

He carefully explained that this decision did not fall within the scope of authority of his committee. He rather suggested that I should get in touch with the moderator and his committee. In other words, I was being referred back to the exact same people where I had originally started. I had gone a full circle.

I then wrote a letter to the chairmen of all these committees suggesting that we have a combined meeting to try and thrash this out. I was assured that I would be given a date. And yet, as we got into the last week before the exam, with only five working days left, I still had not been given a date to meet the chairmen. The situation started becoming very bleak. The students were understandably tense. John Bojé said that he would give each of the children a handheld calculator as a gift to assist them on their way with their matriculation examination. This would uplift their spirits and bolster their determination to write their exams. It was a wonderful idea.

The absence of official approval for the children to write their exams at St Alban's hung over us like a black pall. The students continued their studies. They hoped that it would all come right. At the back of their minds, they must have realised that this might come to nought.

We checked again on the situation at the township schools in Mamelodi. They were closed shut. There was no trace of any army protection or back-up, so even if the children had elected to write their exams in Mamelodi, in their words "under the barrel of the gun", it would not take place. There were no matriculation exams in the townships at all that year. This meant that the children of the townships would be penalised. They would have had to forfeit a whole year of no education and examinations.

With 48 hours to go, we were becoming desperate. Tension had risen. Even wonderful John, always smiling, looked depressed. His face was ashen. He could not face the schoolchildren. He felt that we had let them down. It was a terrible admission and despite it not being his fault at all, he shouldered the blame.

At the same time, Marianne had agreed to attend a women's meeting. This was a gathering of ladies who were concerned about the conflict situation in South Africa. They wanted peace. It was an interesting mix of people ranging from ordinary working middle-class to some upper-class ladies. There were blacks as well as whites. It was an interesting gathering, and it was not often that blacks and whites came together. With this, there seemed to be universal hope for peace and calm in the country.

Something prompted Marianne to tell the gathering of women about the tragic circumstances facing the children from Mamelodi. They would be denied the right to take their examinations. This would mean that they would lose the year. They could not enter the tertiary education institutions for which they desperately longed. There was no guarantee that normal school life would resume at the township schools in the following academic year. The children's career paths and dreams were in tatters.

The group of women were shocked at Marianne's story. They could not believe that children could be penalised in such a brutal way. Some even asked the question about what their reaction would be had this been their very own children and not a bunch of black kids.

One of the ladies present was a Mrs Viljoen. It so happened that her husband was the Minister of Education, that is national education. He was not just responsible for white education but also black education, and all the education departments fell under him.

Mrs Viljoen, like the rest of the ladies present, was dismayed. She promised Marianne that she would tell her husband. She called Marianne later that day and said that I was to call the Minister at 6.00am the next morning. This would be 26 hours before the first examinations were due to take place.

I must confess that I had little hope. I called the Minister at 6.00am the following morning at his private residence on the number Mrs Viljoen had given Marianne. I felt uncomfortable—even fearful. But the Minister promised to look into the matter. He said that we would hear from him within three hours. That meant 9 o'clock that morning and 23 hours before the first exam was due to take place.

The Deputy Minister of Education, Sam de Beer, called just after 8.00am. He gave me the news. The black children of Mamelodi on the Outreach programme had been granted permission to sit for their exams at the white school of St Alban's College.

This was gooseflesh stuff.

My excitement for the children's sake was overwhelming. It meant that with just 24 hours to go, we had at last obtained the official approval. The Minister and his deputy had cut through all the laws of apartheid. They decided to give these children a chance.

Had the right-wing press picked this up at all, there would be a massive outcry. What the Ministers were doing was to fly in direct contravention of the Nationalist government's stated policy of apartheid—it was unbelievable!

There were certain conditions which we had to comply with. These were of an administrative or technical nature. For example, we would have to make special arrangements for the examination papers to be collected at 7.30am from the Department of Education and rushed out to St Alban's College to be there at 8.00am to enable the children to start writing their examinations.

There could be no extensions of time and the examinations had to end at the appointed time, namely three hours later, at 11.00am. More importantly, these completed examination papers had to be returned to the Department of Education by 11.30am.

I asked Djundju whether he would be prepared to accept the important task of collecting the examination questionnaires then delivering the completed answers. Remember, he was one of the students arrested in the 1976 Soweto uprisings.

He readily accepted.

We then had to inform the Department of Education who would be the invigilator. In other words, the person who would sit in the hall each day to keep a watch over the matriculants as they completed their answers.

Sue Clarence, one of the staff members at St Alban's College, readily volunteered. She was delighted to help.

We had to satisfy the Department of Education that there would be one hall dedicated for the purpose of the Mamelodi children for the two-week period that the exams would be written. This we were able to do and over that period, we were able to satisfy the various aspects of invigilation, supervision and venue.

I called John with the exciting news. He was so overtaken with joy that he could not speak. I told him that I would come out to the school and address the children at 1 o'clock that day.

When I arrived at the school and met the children that afternoon, they still did not know the news. They still thought that we were struggling with the various officials at the Department of Education and were already making peace with the fact that this would, in all likelihood, be a hopeless, wasted year. They would have to pack up their things and start heading back to the townships with their tails between their legs.

We had 20 hours to go before the first exam was to be written. I met with the students. The anxiety showed. I could see the sadness on their faces.

"The Minister has granted you permission to write your matric exams, starting tomorrow morning!" I blurted out. I then burst into tears. It was just too much. It was overwhelming.

John also burst into tears—but he gave me a massive bear hug.

The children then started crying; I think simply to release the tension that had been building up over the past few weeks, if not months. Tears turned into joy as the children jubilantly danced around hugging each other. Then they started singing. They gave a big shout. The excitement took over. They were overjoyed and ran off whooping with delight.

That year's pupils all passed their final examinations, and all made it into tertiary education institutions.

Don and President F.W. de Klerk

Don with President Nelson Mandela

Don, Dr Albertina Luthuli and Lungile Luthuli

Desmond and Leah Tutu, with Don and his granddaughter, Jessica MacRobert

Don with 13 of his 16 grandchildren

10 ~ The Women of Soweto

The women of Soweto are tough!

Get Ahead Foundation was starting to make waves by advancing small loans to the poor, with many being illiterate and uneducated. These people could not borrow from the banks. So, we started our group lending schemes, or *stokvels*, which relied on group or peer pressure for the repayment of loans. It worked. Borrowers understood perfectly that their co-borrowers in the group would lean on them to repay. Even our tough chairman, Dr Motlana, reminded them all by saying: "There is no free lunch. Pay back and get a bigger loan to advance further."

Over time, the greater percentage of our borrowers were women. It was awe-inspiring how much hardship they could withstand and still, they were remarkably cheerful, despite all the challenges they faced. They would have to leave early in the morning to go to work. This meant long journeys by bus, train or taxi to the nearest city. From there, they would have to catch another form of transport to their place of employment. Often, they were working as domestic help, or char ladies, and not paid well. At the end of their long day, they would have to make their way back home, sometimes only arriving after dark.

Weekends were then busy with household chores; washing, ironing, cleaning, or going shopping to buy weekly provisions.

Most Sunday mornings were dedicated to church activities. I was moved by how firm the blacks were in their beliefs, and church service could take a long time on Sunday mornings, with everyone fully immersed in the proceedings—an event of note! Sunday afternoons would be reserved for social gatherings and when there would be family parties or get-togethers. The weekend was certainly jam-packed with activities!

There was also a solid core of women who worked from home running their own small businesses. There were a number of dressmakers who would sew clothes then sell them. Others would knit jerseys. Some might make food for sale at taxi ranks where people would queue for their transport. Then there were the shebeens, where people could get together and meet to have a drink.

Townships like Soweto had not made provisions for any entertainment facilities. There were no clubs, and bars and pubs did not exist at all. Liquor laws meant that black people could not open bars and sell liquor—they certainly could not purchase beer and hard spirits from white retail outlets. Despite these prohibitive laws, shebeens sprang up. More often than not, the owner of a shebeen was a lady. They became known as shebeen queens.

It was not easy to get started as a shebeen queen. One first had to consult with the members of their family to get them to agree to convert one of the four rooms of the matchbox house into a public lounge. The budding shebeen queen would then have to let it be known that her home was a place of entertainment where people could relax. More particularly, patrons could buy beer.

To get started, she would have to buy her stock. Nobody would give her credit. Black people could not get loans. So, she had to pay cash for the beer she bought. This meant that it was difficult to get started. She would have to start saving money upfront. Sometimes, she might be able to borrow from other members of the family who would have to be repaid in due course.

Having purchased her stocks of beer, she would need to keep the beers cold. Refrigeration was therefore necessary. However, in her small house, she could not be expected to keep all her stocks of beer in refrigerators. There was just not enough space in the matchbox house. At best, she might have one extra refrigerator in her kitchen and possibly another small one in one bedroom. This meant that every time they needed to replenish a patron's beer, they would have to go to the next room to get to the refrigerator and possibly disturb those in the room. Children might be sleeping in the bedroom.

My friend Dudley introduced me to Sophie Sojane from Soweto. She was a shebeen queen. She told me her story—it was a hard life.

Sophie mentioned that she could not keep all her beer supplies in her house or on her premises. This would be a very unwise thing to do. The reason was quite simple: the police would raid her every now and again because she was running an illegal operation. She was prevented by law from selling alcohol without a liquor license. The laws, and the police, made it almost impossible to obtain this necessary permit and it was one of the hazards of running an illegal operation such as a shebeen. If the police were to raid, which they often did, they could confiscate all the illicit beer and alcohol found on Sophie's premises.

Sophie described a typical police raid.

Patrons of Sophie's Shebeen were settled in, sitting in the lounge. They would be discussing the events of the day or the week. A shebeen was a great meeting place, and Sophie was a good and hospitable hostess, so her venue was popular, with a good spread of patrons.

There would be a loud bang on the door, which would then burst open with policemen forcing their way in. In any event, the front door was always unlocked for patrons. There was no need to be quite so obtrusive, but this was the practice of a policeman. There would be teams of three or four men. Often two white policemen accompanied by two lesser ranked black policemen. The patron's reaction would vary from being uncomfortable to being afraid.

The police would see the liquor on the table. They would charge Sophie for running an illegal liquor outlet. And then they would search the house to find other boxes of beer. They would look for refrigerators. There would be an opening or closing of doors. There would be banging and a loud noise. The patrons and members of the household would be thoroughly disturbed by all this commotion.

The most important thing on a policeman's mind was to find the supply or stores of liquor. They would turn the house upside-down to find these supplies. Once they found them, the liquor would be confiscated. These were to be used as evidence when Sophie would be charged in courts a day or two later. The nature of her charge was that she was running an illegal liquor operation. She did not have a license to sell liquor. She was selling liquor to blacks.

Having removed all the liquor from her house, the police now had enough evidence. They would give her a summons informing her to appear in court two days later. Here, they would produce the offending contraband; the bottles of liquor they had found and removed.

This meant that Sophie's entire stock could be depleted. In balance sheet terms, she could be wiped out. There would be nothing left.

But Sophie was smart.

She had an arrangement in place with her neighbour, a widow. This friendly widow was happy to let Sophie have three refrigerators in her home in which Sophie could store her liquor. This meant that Sophie could have a small supply of beer at her home for patrons as they arrived. As and when further supplies were needed, she, or a child would run next-door and bring a few more bottles back into her house. She naturally had to pay rent to the widow for the storage. That was par for the course. But it meant that her major stocks of beer were safe.

Two days later, Sophie would appear in the Magistrates Court. She would be charged with running an illegal liquor outlet and plead guilty to the charges. There would be an automatic admission of guilt fine. She would pay this. After a while, she regarded this as being part of the running expenses of her business. It became the going rate, and over time she overcame the fear, becoming used to the harassment.

There were long hours for a shebeen queen. Unlike licensed bars and liquor outlets, there were no closing times. While most bars have a closing time of say 11.00pm, this was certainly not the case with Sophie. She could only close once her last patron had left. This was quite testing for her because to make her patrons happy, she would have to be open for as long as they wanted to be there. These could be for long and trying periods of time, not only for Sophie, but also her family members. She gained a good reputation of being open until the early hours of the morning. This was nice for people who had come off shift duty with no work the next day. They could lie in. Sophie could not.

The drinking habits of the patrons was interesting. In most downtown Johannesburg bars or other places around the world, each person would buy her or his own beer. They would then sit and sip it, either quietly on their own, or in the group they were with. From time to time, one of the group would even offer to buy the rest a round of drinks.

This was not the practice in the shebeen. One person would buy a large bottle of beer. A litre of beer. This would then be placed on the table by the purchaser and he would then offer to fill the glasses of those sitting around the room. When his bottle of beer was finished, the next person would buy another litre of beer and place it on the table. People would help themselves as and when their glasses became empty.

Sometimes, one of the fellow patrons might have fallen on hard times. He would not have enough money to buy his round. This did not matter. If he was a regular patron and the other patrons knew him, everyone would be quite happy for him to sit there drinking from their bottles of beer. They knew full well that when his fortunes changed, he would be back, and he would buy a little more than usual to repay the kindness that the fellowship shown to him at that moment. This added to the atmosphere of the shebeen and created a new dimension of social interaction.

In the morning Sophie would spend most of her time cleaning the house and making it neat. She would be preparing for her visitors that evening. It was hard work because some of the previous night's guests left very late, even in the early hours of the morning.

It was on mornings like this, when Sophie was cleaning up, that she would be paid another visit. It would be by an off-duty policeman wearing no mark of officialdom.

But Sophie knew him. He had been on raids to her house in the middle of the night before. He would be very polite. He would ask after her family. How were the children doing at school? He knew she was a widow and asked how she was coping. She said that she was getting on alright. It was a very friendly and courteous meeting. When he left, she offered him a bottle of beer which he graciously accepted.

I tackled Sophie about being so friendly or hospitable to this man who had obviously raided her previously and had cost her financially with her losses of stocks of beer; or the fine that she paid in court. She smiled and said that the visit from this policeman in plain clothes was his way of sending out a message to her. He was signalling her that there would be a raid on her premises in the next two to three nights. This meant that she had to quietly tip off the patrons to not be too upset. For most patrons, this was a regular occurrence and it did not bother them too much. For Sophie, it meant that she had to take the added precaution of ensuring that she had limited stocks of liquor on her premises. To do otherwise would mean that the police could confiscate all that they found when they raided. This could be a huge financial knock.

Sophie explained that the regular raids by the police were a part of the business experience. She had to minimise her losses. But if she played the game correctly, she would survive. Her patrons would admire her for her courageousness. They would come back again. Often in larger numbers.

Sophie's story got better. She started providing food for her patrons. These were simple but good dishes. This added to her popularity. Hers became a highly sought after shebeen. Slowly her fortunes grew.

People living in Soweto could apply for permission to erect a garage for a motor car on their premises. Sophie applied and permission was granted. She then went about erecting the garage, which was constructed in such a way that it served as a larger meeting place for patrons. Once it had opened and was functioning, Sophie's shebeen became even more popular. More patrons could visit. They spent time socialising in the new and expanded building. It also meant that her home was now restored to its original form, the lounge and bedrooms resumed their original functions.

With her increased business, Sophie was able to provide more for her children. As a widow and sole breadwinner, she was able to start providing them with a good education. She wanted the best for her children. After school, she wanted them to attend a tertiary learning institution. This would mean that the children once qualified, could get regular and well-paid jobs.

From very small beginnings she was able to give her children a much better start in life.

11 ~ Strange Laws

Some people went against the grain—some of the whiteys were good guys, and this is how I was introduced to Peter Magano.

I received a letter from Peter, who wrote to me saying that he had been invited to contact me through a mutual friend, Tony Brink. He was not able to find a job and Tony felt that I may be able to help.

In the 1960s, the government introduced legislation banning certain organisations such as the South African Communist Party; ANC; the Pan African Congress (PAC); and others. Not only were these organisations banned, but to be a member of these organisations was a criminal offence. Moreover, if you were seen as promoting the ideals or the objectives of one of these banned organisations, this too was an offence and you could go to jail if found guilty of these offences.

Peter's problem was that he was in prison for 15 years on Robben Island. While this might carry some sort of stigma in normal commercial circles, Peter had added difficulties—serving time with many well-known political activists and prisoners, he was also a fiercely loyal member of the ANC. He made it his duty to persuade township inhabitants by promoting the aims and objectives of the ANC. When considered in the present-day climate, these objectives of the ANC were very plausible. They advocated for equality for all; the protection of civil rights; respect for property; equal education and opportunity for all.

But the government of the day would not accept these notions. Theirs was a policy of white domination. White supremacy. To think that blacks could be equal to whites was unheard of.

Peter had been arrested for promoting the aims and objectives of a banned organisation, the ANC. He was tried before a judge in the High Court and the evidence against him was overwhelming. He was clearly guilty and was sentenced to jail and incarcerated on Robben Island for 15 years.

With the political climate in South Africa being what it was, it was hardly surprising that Peter could not find a job at all. Whites in general and much of the business community lived in fear of the government, and in particular, of the ANC. Being a supporter of the ANC did not help Peter's endeavours to secure employment.

We met, and what a lovely gentleman he was! I met his wife, Salomina, and later, most of their children. We became good friends and worked together for many years.

Peter did not have a driver's license and so, was dependent on public transport like taxis and buses, but he was prepared to walk for the cause. He was prepared to not only walk, but also work for long hours promoting the objectives of our company.

I was grateful to Tony Brink for having introduced us. Indeed, Tony's story is an interesting one. He held a doctorate degree in geology and became Dean of the Faculty of Geology at the Witwatersrand University in Johannesburg.

Tony was passionate about music, and especially loved Gilbert and Sullivan operettas. From the mid-1950s, he would stage an annual production of a Gilbert and Sullivan operetta. These were highly entertaining events! The opening night was a splendid affair—members of the audience were invited to come in black tie, with the men wearing tuxedos and the women dressed in long ballroom gowns. Some even went so far as to have opera glasses.

Sometimes, the opening night was also the closing night. A fair amount of work and seriousness went into the rehearsals. These were held on Sunday nights for the four weeks preceding opening (and closing) night. Lead singers and principals had to learn their words, coupled with a bit of acting. This was not the case for those of us who were members of the chorus—we could hold our music sheets in our hands and sing but we were always described as the "walk-on chorus", with the 'ch' in the word 'chorus' pronounced with a soft 'ch' sound, as opposed to the phonetic 'k'.

Apart from the hilarity of the musical operettas, Tony had a very deep-rooted sense of political correctness. He came from a very liberal background. He hated the laws and the actions of the government of the day.

Each Christmas Eve, he and friends, including my uncle Wilfred and his wife, Marion, would gather opposite the political wing of the Pretoria Central Prison. This was where white political prisoners were kept. Every year, Tony and his group would stand opposite the prison in Pretoria and sing Christmas carols to the political prisoners in their cells.

I joined Tony and the group one Christmas Eve. We sang with gusto. It was a bright, cloudless night. The stars were shining above us.

Having sung two carols, we paused. Then came the reply from the political prisoners. They started singing Christmas carols back to us. Occasionally, we on the outside would join in their songs; on other occasions, we would sing a new carol back to them. And so, the sing-song went back and forth. My friend Hugh Lewin, while in that jail, loved the singing from across the street.

Tony made headlines on one occasion. His domestic lady, Gemina, lived on the premises at his house. Most white South African houses have backrooms or servants' quarters. This was where his domestic lady, Gemina, was staying. Her husband came to stay with her, after work. This was normal as far as Tony was concerned. A man and woman.

The police raided Tony's home one night. They found this man in Gemina's room at the back. The visitor did not have a permit to be at that particular address. His pass book was not endorsed with the name or address of an employer at Tony's address. Technically, he was wrong in the eyes of the law.

The police wanted to arrest him and take him to jail for being a criminal offender. Tony intervened. He said it was totally wrong. He said that it was he, Tony, who had given the man permission to be living there that night. It was, therefore, he, Tony, who should be arrested.

So, the police obliged and arrested Tony. He was taken to the police station, where he spent the night.

The next day he was brought before the Magistrate and charged with an offence under the Group Areas Act. The offence was having Gemina's husband living on the same premises when his pass book did not show that he was legally permitted to be there.

Tony's argument was simple. He said that it was perfectly normal for a man to live with his wife. If the wife had a home or dwelling, then the husband must stay with the wife. It was only natural.

The Magistrate could not find anything wrong with Tony's humane argument, and said so. But he almost apologetically felt that he had to apply the law: technically, Tony was wrong. The Magistrate found him guilty. He imposed a sentence 25 days in jail, or a fine of R25—not a lot of money.

To make the point, Tony elected to go to jail, refusing to pay the small fine. He spent that night in jail, with the press covering this widely. Friends paid the small fine the next day and Tony was released but he had made his point.

Imagine going to jail on a matter of principle? Tony was indeed a brave man!

12 ~ Hawkers

Having spoken about shebeen queens, a word about the illegal traders, or hawkers, might not be amiss.

Because of unemployment, many people became street hawkers. They were hawking their goods from a street pavement. Many of them were women who would strategically place themselves where there was a lot of traffic. This would often be near taxi ranks and bus stops or train stations, where there would be large queues of people waiting to catch taxis to go home or to work.

Their hawking operations provided them with a meagre but useful income. They were able to pay for food for the household and buy clothing for their children with their small earnings.

South Africa's cities are chock-a-block full of hawkers, which, through my travels, I can tell you is a common sight throughout Africa; Nairobi, Kenya and Addis Ababa in Ethiopia also have a significant number of hawkers sitting side-by-side on the curb selling their wares.

Most of these hawkers follow their commercial instincts and trade where there is likely to be the greatest number of customers. This would be at these populated areas such as bus stops, taxi ranks and train stations, but South African laws at the time did not support this segment of income earners and regulated how hawkers could operate under the existing traffic laws.

When I first started working in Soweto, the law was quite clear. A hawker could sell his or her wares in a specific area. This could not just be anywhere. It had to be a defined area. More especially and most frustratingly, the hawker could trade only on that spot—but only for a limited amount of time—for an hour. At the end of that first hour, the hawker had to move on to a new spot, 100 metres away, and could trade at this new spot for the next hour. If they were to comply with the law, they would have to pack up their bananas and oranges, or clothing, or whatever it is that they were trading, into a big bag and lug this to the new spot 100m away.

Well, of course, this didn't happen, and the hawkers simply stayed in the best possible place to trade, close to the taxi ranks, bus stops and train stations. In property terms, you hear developers talk about "location, location, location", so why on earth would any smart trader move 100m away, each hour, from the best spot to trade? It just wasn't practical!

The problem was that the traffic police would start hounding these poor traders. This was because the law said that it was a traffic offence for the traders to stay there for more than one hour, or to be in the incorrectly designated area. When they found an offender, the traffic officers would write out a summons and issue it on the spot to the trader. This meant that she would have to then appear in court on a given day as stated in the summons, and she could not trade further that day. The summons would be issued if she was wrong as to time, or the place of trading.

The hawker would have to go to court in the morning and wait her turn to be called. As with so many of the other courts, the traffic courts were overcrowded. People had to wait many hours before their case was called, and they could appear before the Magistrate.

After being called, it was then an easy matter. They would plead guilty and pay an admission of guilt fine. This meant coughing up what was for them a very scarce resource, namely, money.

Occasionally, it got worse. Some of the traffic inspectors were absolute swines and seemed to enjoy hammering the small traders; the little women whose sole source of income was their small table with its assortment of fruits or vegetables. These policemen would take delight in writing out a summons there and then. They would hand the original to the lady informing her that she must appear in court on a particular day. The copy of the summons was of course kept by the traffic officer. The official would gleefully explain to the poor lady that she would have to be in court by 9.00am on the appointed court day and that she must wait for the matter to be heard. Her heart would sink. This would mean that she could not be at her workstation selling her small groceries. Rather, she would have to use up her hard-earned money to pay for a taxi to get her from Soweto the court in downtown Johannesburg. She would then have to hang around all day until she was called to appear before the Magistrate. She would plead guilty. The Magistrate would hand down the sentence, usually a fine of R100. This might not have been much to some people but to the poor lady from Soweto it was a fortune; representing a number of days takings at her small table. This was a big loss in financial terms.

Yet, she would bravely pay the R100 fine and the next morning, she would be back at her spot selling her fruit and vegetables. Somehow, she realised that the police interference and bullying, coupled with the taxi fares and fines, which all ate into her hard-earned cash, were part of the business expenses. These hawkers were truly remarkable in their philosophical way of life. Rarely would they rise up in anger. Occasionally, they might argue with the traffic officer.

But these traffic officers could be even worse. Sometimes, they had a real mean streak and could be truly harsh—rather than issuing the hawker with a summons which would command her to appear in court on a particular day, the traffic officers occasionally plundered the small table of the hawker. They would confiscate all the products on display and take all the bananas, oranges, tomatoes, apples. This meant that the lady lost her entire stock. It was like one's factory being wiped out: all the assets were gone.

The worst was to follow.

These traffic officers would then pour the lady's fruit and vegetables into the gutter or trample them into the ground. They would stamp on the bananas, oranges, tomatoes—destroying them by squashing them. The poor lady was dismayed to see her stock being destroyed before her very eyes by such cruel people.

We would protest to the authorities if we heard about these practices. However, the traders were too scared of the police to ever give us their names. We would lodge a general complaint with the chief traffic officer but nothing ever really came of our objections.

On one occasion, when Peter telephoned from Brits, a town to the west of Pretoria and Johannesburg, he said that the policemen there were taking the fruit and vegetables of the hawkers who were trading on the side of the road.

They would pour these into the gutters and then stamp all over them. Peter said I should go and have a word with the commanding officer of the police station. He said that we were not dealing with the traffic police, who were supposed to look after motor cars and motor traffic, but the regular police who were supposed to keep law and order.

Here they were embarking on these sad and malicious practices of destroying the entire wares of a small trader.

I had no hard evidence. However, Peter assured me that this was the case. He could bring in ladies who had lost everything. He would accompany and reassure them that they would not be prosecuted.

I said that it was not necessary for Peter to bring the ladies to begin with. Rather, let me have a word with the commanding office of the Brits police station. Let me sound him out. If necessary, we could bring in the ladies and the evidence later on.

I went to the Brits police station, I asked a young sergeant if the commanding officer was there. He replied affirmatively. He went and asked the commanding officer if I could have a meeting with him. He returned after a very short while saying that the commanding officer would see me then and there. I was ushered into his office. He was certainly a big and tough looking chap, and he towered above me. As we shook hands, I noticed that his big hand was much larger than mine.

He inquired how he could be of assistance. I explained to him that we were trying to help create small businesses. A lot of our people were ladies who traded as hawkers.

They traded at popular spots such as taxi ranks, bus stops and near train stations. They were aiming at passers-by. They sold a wide range of goods from clothing to fruit and vegetables. I mentioned that we had received a report that police officers from the Brits police station, his police station, were upending the trays and tables of the small hawkers then trampling the fruit and vegetables into the ground. This meant that the goods were totally destroyed. I explained that the ladies had paid hard cash to get their basic stock. They had small margins when they resold the goods. For them to lose their entire stock in this way was a total disaster.

I also mentioned that in selling their goods, the ladies would eke out a small pittance from which they could pay for food or even clothes for their children. I suggested that by their actions, the police would create considerable animosity towards themselves. People would not look to the police for help in enforcing law and order. Instead, they were seen to be the destroyers of small enterprises. The reputation of the police would be tarnished and would leave much to be desired.

The commanding officer on duty at the Brits police station turned out to be Captain Johan Nothnagel. His face grew stern as I told him the story. I realised that I might be creating trouble. I thought that I would have to adopt a slightly more cautious approach to make sure that Captain Nothnagel did not instruct his junior officers to become even more proactive and go on a witch hunt after the poor hawkers.

To my surprise, Captain Nothnagel said that he agreed with my sentiments. He said that he had recently returned from an international police convention in the United States where he was sent over as one of the selected police officers from South Africa. It was at this conference that speakers, and their audiences, appreciated the need to work closely with communities and not antagonise them. Thus, the police should be seen to be working in harmony with the community. In this way, they could be tipped off as to where serious crimes were taking place, and who the criminals might be. They could also be given an early warning on proposed future criminal activities. The community was seen to be a vital link in information gathering as well as maintaining law and order.

The captain explained this to me and said that the actions of the junior officers were clearly not in line with what they had heard at the international convention in the USA. Rather, the actions of his junior officers would result in hostility as well as sever communication. He complained that many of the junior staff were "white trash", to use his words. These were people who could often not find a regular job in the outside world. They thought that by joining the police, they could secure a salary, at least, and that for most of the time the job of being a bobby on the beat was a cushy one. They were not often called on to investigate major crimes but were active in policing petty crime, and this a normal day's work.

Captain Nothnagel surprised me by saying that he would look into the matter and would take serious steps against those junior officers who had performed these sad deeds. He surprised me further by saying that he would telephone me to give me a report back. This was surprising because often, when faced with charges against their own personnel, my experience was that the police may have noted the particulars of the complaint but never gave a follow-up report, particularly as to whether they had ever done anything about investigating the cause of the complaint. I left the meeting with Captain Nothnagel feeling that here, at long last, was a small glimmer of hope that we might be able to shift perceptions.

Before leaving him, I noted that he had a bird book on his table. This was a guide to birding written by a well-known ornithologist. I was again slightly surprised that this may have found its way onto his desk and asked him if he was keen birder. He indicated that he was. Being located in Brits, which was a small town in the country, there were quite a few birds in the area. He relaxed by going on walks through the veld and bush, and seemed to enjoy looking at and identifying the birds which he saw on his outings.

True to his word, Captain Nothnagel telephoned a week or so later. He said that his investigations had shown that two new recruits were the culprits. He told me that he had spoken seriously to these junior officers and explained how the ladies had lost their entire savings through the criminal acts of the policemen. He used their actions to show how they could alienate the local population and thereby make their own job as policemen more difficult. He went on to tell these young men how important it was to establish a good relationship with the local community and its people.

Captain Nothnagel was certainly not the ordinary role model of a white policeman, and I was pleased when he shortly thereafter received a promotion to the South African Police Service head office in Pretoria. It was not long before he called me again and we resumed contact, which eventually grew into a good friendship.

13 ~ Hawkers – USA

The story about the hawkers and their harassment goes further—the board talked about it at a meeting held in the USA at the office of Senator Kennedy. When two of the board members, Maurice Tempelsman and Ambassador David Miller, asked pointedly what could they, sitting in the USA, do to help the poor? I touched on the hawkers and their harassment, but in particular, the amount of red tape facing a very small businessman starting a new business from scratch.

The red tape was horrific for a start-up business person. The number of forms, delays and rejections were unbelievable. The well-known economist, Hernando de Soto, illustrated how problematic this was by explaining the situation in his country, Peru. He related how the government there hated the informal sector traders; so much so, they were described or classified as being communists. His investigations showed that these people were far from being communists and were aspiring to be small capitalists. All they wanted to do was have their own businesses. De Soto pointed out to his country's government that these aspiring business people, mainly women, wanted loans or venture capital to start their businesses, and to own a small piece of ground which they could offer as security to the banks who offered loans. The position for South African blacks was exactly the same as that of Peruvians.

At that USA board meeting, both Maurice and David again offered to do something. In a very quiet voice, Ambassador Miller said that with the change in government in the USA, he, as a Republican had been invited again to serve on the US government's National Security Council. He said: "I know Niël Barnard."

That name rang many bells. Everybody knew Niël Barnard in South Africa. He was the head of the country's National Intelligence Service, but he was a faceless person and shied away from the spotlight and press. Despite this, we knew he was working to dismantle the hated security laws and practices. David suggested we write a letter to Niël to tell him about the red tape facing the country's hawkers, and that the little people were not communists as the South African government thought.

"Please use my name," he said.

On our return to South Africa, I asked Marianne how I could go about finding this Barnard bloke. Nobody knew where to find him. He was never seen publicly. But he was pulling some strings!

Until, one evening, Marianne and I had been invited to the Japanese Embassy. The Japanese had become great supporters of programs helping small businesses, including our little company, Get Ahead. All the embassies in South Africa had a visitors' book, which you had to sign as you left the Embassy. Two names above mine in the visitors' book was Niël Barnard, and he gave his Edward Street address. Wow! That was only a couple of streets away from me. I wrote a letter to Niël at his Edward Street address, asking very politely whether I could meet him, at the suggestion of Ambassador Miller in Washington D.C. I handed in the letter at the Edward Street address, and as expected, there were many security people hanging around in addition to tight security measures. I handed the letter to the security man. Within an hour, my telephone rang, with the speaker saying, "Hello Donald, this is Maritz Spaarwater. Niël Barnard has asked me to set up a meeting so we can meet. Does tomorrow suit?"

Maritz was polite and courteous—unlike so many big, white South African businessmen who can never make their own telephone calls, always believing their importance is magnified by the amount of time his secretary can keep you, the listener, hanging on to the telephone.

The polite telephone call from Maritz was very welcoming—except that he called me by my full name and not the abbreviated 'Don'. This was a mere formality after getting to know him when he was a young man employed by my grandfather's law firm at the same time as the young F.W. de Klerk. F.W.'s father, Senator Jan de Klerk, advised Maritz and F.W. to join a Scottish firm as opposed to an English firm. That was a throwback from the time when the English fought against the Boers. Of course, F.W. de Klerk eventually went on to become the President of South Africa who unbanned all the opposition parties and released political prisoners like Nelson Mandela.

I had a productive meeting with Maritz at Schoeman Street in Pretoria. As we chatted amicably, I wondered how many tapes would be buzzing around recording our meeting, exactly as had happened when the Special Branch had asked me to meet Hugh Lewin at Pretoria's high-security prison a few blocks away. I mentioned to Maritz that I was not a communist as the security bureaucrats had labelled me. On the contrary, the objectives of our company, including the well-meaning personalities on the board, were to help the poor; give a hand to the small businesspeople, especially the women who created jobs and employment to feed their children.

We were generating many success stories and gaining recognition by international governments and embassies who supported us. I mentioned that we often organised tours to Soweto, Mamelodi and other townships, and that the foreign embassies were only too happy to come along. That helped us with building our profile and securing funding. I was taken aback when he requested that embassy personnel arriving from overseas come on our tours before following the protocols of introducing themselves to South African government representatives.

Blacks were appalled at the rather slimy and underhanded ways in which the US government operated and how they continued to do business with South Africa while being aware of the government's oppression of black people and abuses of human rights. They saw no hope of introducing any changes to the system.

The USA and its governmental hierarchy had begun implementing a strange policy towards South Africa. That policy was known as 'constructive engagement', and its thrust was to send a message to South Africa and its apartheid government that the USA did not condone South Africa's policies towards blacks. It was an attempt by the Americans to try change South Africa from within—to change inner thought processes and laws, and it got me thinking.

Here I was, a tiny cog in the wheel, talking to one of the most powerful men in the country about the sad state of affairs facing our downtrodden people.

Even more amazing was that the tentacles of government, on both sides, knew intimately the inner workings of how certain people in high places advised on and responded to information—such as on the plight and secrets of the oppressed black population. The fear factor was real. No wonder I objected to having my telephone being bugged and my mail being intercepted!

During apartheid in South Africa, this was standard operating procedure, and while the government of the day was known to influence the political ongoings of other countries, much like what transpired during the US elections in 2016, we will likely never know the true extent of how this has impacted the everyday person on the street. What we do know is that oppressive political regimes that are morally questionable can only survive for so long before the will of the people takes over.

14 ~ USA Government Veto

I was overjoyed when, in early 1984, I was approached by representatives from USAID in South Africa. They had heard we were creating jobs in Soweto for the unemployed and starting up small businesses and wanted 'in'.

We were targeting the bottom end of the economy where people were hurting most as a result of racial inequality, with lay-offs taking place in the mainstream economy. USAID said we should consider an agreement with them, and hence the US government. What they proposed was funding to cover some of the salaries of loan staff operating in the field, as well as grant funding for lending purposes.

What was particularly attractive was that USAID were proposing a multiple-year contract. This was music to our ears. So often, donors would give us a once-off grant and feel that they had done their bit for us, or society, but it would wreak havoc with planning and budgeting. We were never certain from one year, or even one month to the next whether we would have repeat donations, or what was necessary to ensure a constant and regular cash flow. We were living on a knife's edge when it came to paying month-end salaries and expenses, particularly if one or two of the larger donors were a little bit behind or slow in making their payments.

So, this concept of a multiple-year grant was superb—in my mind anyway. I was therefore keen to continue these discussions with USAID. As the process developed, it seemed they might also support us with expertise in microcredit; people who had earned their spurs in micro-lending programmes in other countries. This was yet another plus.

USAID said they would prepare a basic concept document, which would form the basis of an agreement, and get back to me fairly soon.

True to their word, USAID produced a proposal that would eventually end up as a five-year agreement between USAID and Get Ahead—fantastic!

USAID proposed that they would make money available for loans to the emerging informal sector business people of Soweto and other townships. We were compelled to expand our operations to places like Cape Town, Durban, East London and Port Elizabeth. To do this, USAID would also make provisions for salaries of our field staff who were granting loans to the small entrepreneurs. This was big stuff.

USAID also proposed that we would have the support of experts such as Mike Farbman, who eventually became the head honcho of the USAID programme, and Hank Jackelen. Hank was originally from Brazil but educated in the US and had vast experience in micro-finance programmes in many countries. We were to benefit considerably from these two gentlemen and starting in 1984, my friendship with Hank stretched over many years, with repeat visits being made on both sides of the ocean between New York and Johannesburg. Later on, Hank would assist Mike and also help others start another community bank.

The USAID representatives met with Dr Motlana and me over an early morning breakfast at the Carlton Hotel in Johannesburg. USAID outlined the proposal, and I had to keep quiet and mask my excitement. Dr Motlana gave it very serious consideration and said that he would have to take it to our board meeting for their consideration and approval. The board meeting would be in about four weeks. We promised we would get back to USAID as soon as we had met with the board.

Through so-called 'constructive engagement' with South Africa, the US government believed that pressure could be brought to bear on South Africa's government to change its abhorrent racial policies, which the US government in no way condoned. Guided by the Sullivan Principles, the US government felt that through their constructive engagement policy, including meetings and ongoing dialogue, they would be able to change South Africa's apartheid regime. The main man tasked with this responsibility for the US government was the Assistant Secretary of State for African Affairs, Dr Chester Crocker. He had acquired a wide knowledge base through experience in other countries and would be dealing directly with the South African government.

Our board meeting took place four weeks later at the home of Dr Motlana. There was the usual high attendance. All the board members were present, barring Bishop Desmond Tutu, who was away overseas on some church business. This meant that we had 90% attendance at that meeting.

Dr Motlana asked me to outline the proposal of the US government. I did so in full, explaining the proposals. I was quite excited! I was confident that we would have overwhelming support for the adoption of this contract, which would mean a huge shot in the arm for Get Ahead. We could reach out to thousands more and expand our operations to different black townships. We could bring help and hope to so many poor people.

But it was not to be. There was an overwhelming vote against the adoption of this contract with USAID. I was shocked and could not believe my ears as speaker after speaker voiced their disapproval and urged for the non-adoption of this contract.

I didn't take part in the debate. This was way beyond me—I could not understand the nuances of the discussion as it went along very much in a one-way direction.

I stressed to the board members that we needed more funding to expand our operations. How could we do this if we continued to struggle financially? We could reach out to so many of the poor and help the downtrodden. We could create more jobs with people working from their homes and could bring financial relief to so many people.

The reasons for this overwhelming rejection slowly emerged: the problem was with the US government and its policies towards South Africa.

The attitude of blacks was quite clear—constructive engagement was seen by them as a way for the US government to be in bed with the South African government. The US government never publicly criticised South Africa's government for its terrible racial laws and practices. Individual members of the cabinet responsible for perpetuating apartheid weren't ever chastised or even questioned; neither were government leaders who made public statements about the ongoing will of the white people to oppress black people.

There was never any criticism against any of the apartheid laws by the US government. In effect, black people felt that the US government had resorted to its own racist policies, which it had espoused and practised before the introduction of its Civil Rights Act in 1964. Here, Rosa Parks was mentioned on more than one occasion. We were reminded how, in December 1955, in Montgomery, Alabama, she refused to sit at the back of the bus, which was reserved for blacks. She was tired after a day's work and opted to sit in the front few seats that were first-come-first-served but refused to move when the bus became full and was told to do so by the bus driver. She was turfed off the bus. This led to massive bus boycotts and marches in Alabama, to begin with, which spread through the US.

During the board meeting, I heard, for the first time, of the debate that had been raging on over the decisions by some of the US courts on racial practises. The first was the Plessy v. Ferguson case, which ruled that segregated public facilities were legal. A court ruled that there could be separate facilities given to blacks provided these facilities were equal. Thus, the policy of 'separate but equal' became accepted at the turn of the 20th century in the US.

Many years later, this was overturned following the Brown v. Board of Education in Topeka, Kansas, when the US Supreme Court ruled that "separate meant unequal". It was a complete reversal of the Plessy case. My eyes and ears were opened. I had not realised how carefully and meticulously our black leaders had followed the events of the US racial struggle.

The board's vote was unanimous: we just could not be signatories to any agreement with the US government—however lucrative or beneficial the conditions of the contract may be. We could not let the black people down by being party to a deal with a dishonest broker.

And so, I had to tell USAID that, as attractive as the contract would appear to be, our company had, regrettably, turned it down. I had to be very clear in conveying the sentiments of the board and did so by providing a detailed summary of some of their comments, which I gave to USAID. My heart was heavy because it would have made our lives so much easier if we had been able to get this money and the back-up that went with the contract.

The USAID representatives were very disappointed when I told them. Like me, they had believed that this would be a great opportunity and could be a huge step for black small business. Many more jobs would be created despite the hostile and adverse political climate.

I felt despondent. I could fully appreciate all the reasons given by our board members and did not disagree with them. My despondency was caused by the fact that we couldn't deliver to the poor people on a much bigger scale—I felt that I was letting them down. I could not look another poor person in the eyes. How was I to explain this to so many aspirant business people wanting to work from their homes?

They of course knew very little about the proposed contract. In fact, no-one outside the board had any inkling of this big USAID contract from the US government. Nevertheless, I would have to tell these people that we might not be able to lend them money, only because the demands made on us were so great that we did not have enough to extend any further loans. With our ongoing refusal to lend money, these people might not be able to buy food, or clothe their children, or pay school fees.

It was a very dark period in my work in Soweto.

Then, surprisingly, US President Ronald Reagan came to our assistance. This may seem very strange. How could the President of the United States of America and the leader of its government, with its policy of constructive engagement, ever be seen to have come to the rescue of the poor in Soweto, or our tiny little outfit, for that matter?

It worked like this: President Reagan was the leader of the Republican Party, who was voted into the presidency by the people of the United States. Yet, the majority of the people in the Senate were members of the opposition party, the Democratic Party. The Democrats were already known to be more liberal and on the political left—an important factor when it came to South Africa's historical racial laws. Many of the Democrat leaders were vociferous in their condemnation of the policies of the day that were operating in South Africa, likening these to the anti-Semitic practices of Nazi Germany that prevailed in the 1930s.

The Senate decided to propose a law that would mean the application of sanctions against South Africa. It made clear that this was because of the racial laws of our country and, once passed, the law would mean that the US government and corporations could not deal with South Africa. It would be aimed at certain key areas, such as defence, sport and education.

The counterargument from the Republicans was that sanctions would hurt the country economically, and would mean that the worst affected would be the people at the bottom of the economic ladder, namely the poor. It was they who would suffer most if sanctions were to be invoked against South Africa—we would consistently hear this argument over time.

The legislation went to the vote and was passed by Congress because of the Democratic majority, meaning the US government now had to start applying sanctions to South Africa.

However, according to US law, the president has the right to veto any legislation passed by Congress. Therefore, he can reject laws and that with which he does not agree. So, President Reagan elected to veto the legislation, meaning that the US government would not apply sanctions against our government and country.

This produced a remarkable reaction from our board members in Soweto. They wanted an urgent meeting. We called for an unscheduled meeting at the home of Dr Motlana. Our next meeting was still a good two months away. Yet, here was the board wanting to meet as soon as possible.

I was puzzled. Why the sudden urgency now to have a board meeting?

I hardly prepared any papers for the board meeting because we had convened recently; when the board voted out the USAID proposal.

We all arrived very punctually at Dr Motlana's home. We were given tea, but unlike previous occasions, there were no preliminary discussions about ongoing political happenings—we launched into the board meeting straight away.

Jimmy Sojane was first to speak. It was he who had called for this unscheduled meeting. He spoke clearly, reminding us how we had unanimously rejected the big contract offer offered to us by USAID.

Now, however, the American nation had spoken through the US Congress that constituted the House of Representatives and Senate, which most notably held the Electoral College. America's people had voted for sanctions. The vote was quite clear—representing the American nation, it sent a very strong message to the South African government. They had called for sanctions by the US government against South Africa and its government. This was what the black people wanted to hear. They were very grateful to this resolution and the message which it had sent. It gave black people hope. It was quite apparent that the majority of the US people were not in favour of their government's policy of constructive engagement. Rather, the US people felt that more drastic action needed to be taken against the South African government.

President Reagan had exercised his veto. However, he was now in a lame duck situation and would be out of office shortly. The American nation would then express itself on his handling of the desperate situation in South Africa.

There was hardly any further discussion. The board, having previously voted unanimously against the USAID contract, were happy with the US Senate's vote and because of this, we could accept the terms of the USAID contract.

The voting was again unanimous. The meeting was over within 45 minutes, and I was overjoyed.

15 ~ The Board

There was a detailed discussion that took place at one of our meetings. Dr Motlana, Dikgang Moseneke, Tubs Mathabathe and the other well-known political leaders were advancing a very interesting theory of how the abuse of the rule of law in the courts was being used to squash the opposition.

The tools and weaponry at the disposal of the government were far-reaching and wide-ranging, with one of these measures being the detainment of people without trial. Initially, these detentions were for periods of 90 days; subsequently, the period was extended to 180 days, meaning that one could effectively dispose of opposition people for up to half a year.

But that might not always be sufficient. It would be far better to side-line vigorous anti-apartheid leaders for much longer.

A long jail sentence was always forthcoming, and this could be done where these leaders were known members of organisations such as the Communist Party, or the ANC, or the PAC, and if it could be proved that one was a member of any of these banned organisations or seen to be promoting their objectives.

This happened to some of our good friends who were fellow workers at Get Ahead—people like Peter Magano, John Nkosi, Pro Molefe, Julian Motsepe, any one of the Robben Island Old Boys' Club.

The government was always watching. It had its eyes, ears and spies all around. Post was being intercepted. Telephones were being tapped. Ours were!

One evening in Soweto, a protest meeting was held at the only suitable venue we could find; the Regina Mundi Catholic Church, which could accommodate big crowds. Many protest meetings were held here, and Bobby Kennedy once addressed a packed hall of thousands at the church.

During the meeting, Dr Motlana explained how it was not uncommon for him to be arrested straight after having made a rabble-rousing speech at a large gathering at the Regina Mundi hall. He was always very outspoken. He was often angry at the government and would hurl abuse at them.

After some of these loud and rowdy protest meetings, once he had made his speech from the podium, there would be a tap on his shoulder. Somebody would indicate that a person was waiting to see him outside the hall. He would leave the gathering, go outside and would be whisked away by the Special Branch. They had wired the hall and loud-speaking devices. The police were sitting around the corner in their vans listening to everything that was being said. They were recording and taping all the conversations. These tapes would later be used in various court cases, where political leaders would be charged with some or other political offence. And of course, the guy sitting right in front jumping up and down to cheer the speakers on, was wired up and catching all the speeches and remarks. He was broadcasting directly to the security vans outside.

The apartheid government decided that one of the most effective ways of effectively removing vociferous, political anti-government leaders from society was by charging them with treason.

If one were ever found guilty of treason, there was a strong possibility that the accused would be given the death penalty. It became quite common for some of the judges of the High Court to be referred to as "hanging judges". If the State could prove the charge of treason against the accused, these judges were known to impose the death sentence.

Quite often, the charges were far-fetched and proceedings were substantially flawed. The defence counsel could easily knock holes through the attorney-general's case.

Yet, the risk was always there. No-one in any court case could be certain of the outcome—anything could go wrong in a court of law. Being charged with treason meant that the accused could not afford to make one mistake because this might lead to being found guilty, with worse to follow.

To elaborate on Dr Motlana's point, which was to become well-recognised in the late 1980s, the State had found a new tool whereby it could quell the voices of protest from political leaders. Permanently. All you needed was one rather right-wing judge; a prosecution team of two or three State prosecutors; and the Special Branch to provide leading evidence. One could then lay a blanket treason charge against multiple co-accused at the same time.

This would then knock out those accused for at least two to three years, or even much longer. These cases went on for years.

Being charged with treason also meant many leading human rights lawyers would also be taken out of action for a period of time. People like Arthur Chaskalson, George Bizos, David Soggott, Gilbert Marcus, and Sydney Kentridge were always in the courts defending people who were accused of these trumped-up treason charges.

It certainly was a very effective weapon used by the State's ruling government, and it became part of its arsenal.

Many books were written about treason charges. Helen Joseph's book, *If this be Treason*, was a cynical question being asked of the State prosecution teams. She was a very brave lady and had been subjected to house arrests and banning, and even had a flimsy charge of treason brought against her that she had to defend vigorously because of the dire consequences she would face had she lost.

House arrests were another form of effectively removing the opposition. The government would slap an order on a person confining them to their house. They could not leave the magisterial district where their house was situated without the permission of the Magistrate. They had to report on a weekly basis to the police at the local police station, who would in effect be keeping a watch over them. This was merely an administrative order made by the Minister of Justice. He would do so when tipped off by the security police, where there may be insufficient evidence to charge a person with the tougher offence of treason. It was certainly an effective way of stifling individuals. There was no chance to appeal if one was served with such a house arrest order. That was it—they could not leave their home, not even to seek employment. Some of these house arrest orders were challenged in the courts. Almost all were unsuccessful. The government had tightened up its security legislation so much that laws were in place to give administrative orders at any time. There was no question of any hearing as to the rights or wrongs of the matter.

Another effective means of stifling the voices of opponents was to impose a banning order on them. This prohibited one from making any speeches, or even attending public gatherings or meetings, and they could certainly not be quoted in the press.

Sometimes, a political leader would be served with a banning order in addition to being placed under full house arrest. Here, they would be confined to their homes and prohibited from receiving more than one guest at a time. Not being able to leave their home, they depended on the earnings of other family members, or handouts and donations from friends. These were shocking conditions under which to live.

The first time I met Winnie Mandela, then the wife of Nelson Mandela, was when she was subjected to a full house arrest with a banning order. But they went even further with Mrs Mandela. They confined her to a house in Brandfort; a place she had never been to before.

The problem was compounded for Winnie.

Winnie was born in the Transkei in the Eastern Cape. Her home language was Xhosa. She and Nelson had lived in their small home in Vilakazi Street in Soweto, where I often visited. But Brandfort, the little village where she was now under house arrest, was in a completely different part of the country and people there spoke Setswana—quite different to Winnie's home language.

I came to meet her because her brother-in-law, Gilbert Xaba, worked with us at Get Ahead. Gilbert's wife was Winnie's sister.

Although she was subjected to the fluctuations of being an effective political leader, Winnie's bravery in challenging the system could never be doubted.

Political leaders on the board of Get Ahead had described how they had been subjected to the government's form of detention without trial. They were often put in solitary confinement for 90 days, and sometimes, for 180 days.

The security police would arrest them and interrogate them, and ask questions like: "Do you know anything about the ANC?" and, "Is Mr X a member of the ANC?" or, "Were Mr X or Mrs Y furthering the objectives of the ANC?"

Assuming that your responses to these questions posed by the Special Branch were negative, they might then say: "Oh well, we will put you away for a while and you can reflect on your answers."

They would then put you in solitary confinement for 90 days. You were locked up in a cell all by yourself. You had no one to talk to. There was no means of communicating with the outside world. Your food was pushed through a hatch in the door which was opened twice a day. The wardens who came to give you your food and take away your empty plates or your toilet bucket never spoke to you.

All that you might have, if you were lucky, was a bible.

Our friends and the board of directors at Get Ahead described their different ways and means of overcoming the terrible effects of solitude, loneliness and boredom, which all led to depression. At times, they were depressed and even cried in self-pity. Tears flowed down their cheeks. They openly admitted this.

They told stories of how some of their fellow political friends brought out after months of solitary confinement who had 'cracked'. They spilt the beans, which was precisely what the Special Branch were waiting for. In this way, they were able to gather up more information and feed it into their system. They could then start charging other people with treason and bring house arrest or banning order applications against them.

Despite some of her mood swings, Winnie was held in great esteem by many black people and certainly revered by their youth. This is because she never cracked under the system, even after serving a total of 18 months in solitary confinement.

When I met her in Brandfort, I was amazed at her resilience and positive disposition. Despite being the subject of a banning order and being placed under house arrest in an area that was totally foreign to her, she was remarkably chipper!

Visiting Winnie in that small house in Brandfort was a noteworthy experience.

Together with Gilbert and Mike Quawe, a colleague at Get Ahead, three of us had driven to visit her. But the effect of a banning order was that she could not have more than one visitor in her home at a time. Having two or more visitors in one's home would constitute a public gathering and be in breach of the banning order.

When we got to Winnie's little matchbox home in Brandfort, we would have to go in one by one. Each of us would have to visit her and speak with her on our own.

Gilbert, being her brother-in-law, went in first. Then it was my turn. Halfway through our discussion, she asked me: "How many of you are there in the car?" I replied that there were three of us. "Bugger that!" she said. "Why don't you all come in at the same time?"

Such was her disdain for the apartheid government's laws that she was even prepared to defy the conditions of her banning order, knowing that had she been caught, she would have to go back to jail again.

Like so many other leaders, Winnie described the Nationalist's regime as being illegal and completely lacking in any democratic foundation.

On the way back in the car, we were quite spirited. We were impressed at the work which Winnie was doing. She had started a small clinic in the black township outside Brandfort because none existed, and she had become well-accepted and respected by the local people.

Sadly, it was in later years when she was surrounded by the infamous Mandela Football Club that she would become the subject of a number of court cases.

As we approached Soweto, I realised that we, too, had been guilty of an offence. It was also an offence for us to break the terms of Winnie's banning order restricting her to one visitor at a time.

"My goodness!" I thought. "Here we go again!"

Winnie's solitary confinement was highlighted by international media when Senator Edward Kennedy visited her at her little house in Brandfort. It was broadcast on television, radio and well-documented in the press across the world. Senator Kennedy and his entourage, including members of the Mandela family, made a point of rigidly sticking to the banning order. They went in one by one. The television visuals clearly showed Senator Kennedy going into the house alone then coming out by himself.

Get Ahead's board meetings in Soweto were very exciting! Firstly, the chairman, Dr Motlana, insisted that everyone had to be present at each of the four meetings in a year. Secondly, the talk before the board meeting was also interesting, with a lot of security information being passed around; the black mayor of Soweto, Ike Mogasi, was on the run from the Special Branch and they couldn't find him. But someone mentioned that he was hiding in the crypt in a downtown cathedral in a white area.

Dr Motlana would announce: "I have been to see our leader. Please send out the message to all that the leader is strong and healthy," referring of course to Nelson Mandela in prison on Robben Island. All those present knew to get the bush telegraph system active.

After Nelson, it was expected that Thabo Mbeki would be his successor, and the second democratically elected president—this was said long before 1990.

But a problem arose for Dr Motlana. He had been invited by the World Health Organization (WHO) to deliver a speech in Cairo, Egypt. No problem. Except, the government did not issue passports to blacks. So, he was given a temporary passport that was valid for only five days and restricted to just one country: Egypt.

The discussion went on to Chief Albert Luthuli, the former president of the banned ANC, who, likewise, had a five-day passport issued to him to enable him to go to Oslo, Norway, to receive the Nobel Peace Prize—he was the first African to be accorded with that honour. I was lucky to work for the Luthuli family, and the Chief's daughter, Dr Albertina Luthuli.

On one occasion, Desmond Tutu, who was now the Archbishop, had shown his limited passport on television, saying that his nationality was described as being 'undecided'. He scolded the government for doing this when others around the world had their countries of origin shown, such as Irish, or German, or French. The Archbishop stated that he was "stateless" in the country of his birth.

16 ~ Funerals

Funerals are always a sad affair.

Funerals in townships are quite different and are a much larger, livelier affair than the small and sombre funerals of white people that I've been to. Hundreds of people attend a township funeral. People who may be complete strangers to the deceased will come because they know one of the family members and would like to pay their respects to the bereaved.

Word gets out that the main funeral proceedings will be held at a particular hall and people arrive in big buses. It has to be a very big hall because of the number of people in attendance. People from other centres are told where the buses will be leaving from, and at what time, and taxis and other vehicles descend on the hall or church for the funeral.

Quite often, the main funeral in the hall may have been preceded by a small family get-together at the family home. This would have been attended by only a few family members and close friends; a priest or pastor would also be there.

After this, there is the big ceremony in the hall that is then followed by the procession of cars taking the deceased to the cemetery.

The big funeral gathering in the hall is a very important occasion. Unlike so many funerals in white cities, but much like their church services, funerals in the townships go on for a long time. An agenda handed out at the doorway tells you who is the master of ceremonies and the likely order of events.

This order of events is often changed as the mood takes people.

Typically, the order of events would contain an opening prayer said by the priest. Then there is a word of welcome by the master of ceremonies, usually a close friend of the family who thanks everybody for coming to pay their respects to the deceased and the deceased's family. This is followed by the singing of a hymn by a choir. There could also be more than one choir as other choir groups may join in.

Even though funeral proceedings are a sad moment, the choir's singing is very moving and uplifting and interspersed on the agenda or the order of proceedings.

I've always loved the harmony achieved by the voices of African choirs and their joyous hymns, especially. Many black people sing well and have a good ear, and I believe they can speak so many languages because of this ability.

Members of the family would then pay their tributes, followed by close friends and possibly business associates or other connected people. These speeches are also interspersed throughout the agenda.

At the funeral services I normally attend in white cities, it would at most be two, possibly three tributes or eulogies paid to the diseased.

This is not so among my black friends.

What I also found interesting is that even though a particular person may have been regarded as somewhat of a scoundrel, there will still be a massive turnout for his funeral. People would always say good things about him. He knows that he will leave this earth with good messages and blessings. One such funeral I attended in Johannesburg recently was that of the late Gavin Reilly, a former chairman of one of the largest companies in South Africa, Anglo American. The St Martin's Church was filled to the point of overflowing. A second hall was arranged. There was an electronic screening of the service to those in the nearby church hall.

Gavin was a wonderful person. He was outstanding as a business leader. Not only had he headed up the biggest company in South Africa, which was a major world player in the diamond and gold markets, but he had also been a leader in other ways.

It was he who in the mid-1980s led a bunch of businessmen to meet the ANC in exile in Lusaka, Zambia. The then-president, P.W. Botha, was very angry.

It was the start of what was to become a succession of many visits paid by different South African groups to the ANC in exile in Zambia.

I had a soft spot for Gavin. Apart from attending the same dinners, or going to the theatre or opera together, he was also very good to us at Get Ahead—not only did he stroke my feathers from time to time and encourage me to keep going, but he put his money where his mouth was. When I wrote to Jane, his wife, sending my condolences to the family, I mentioned that he had been a very generous individual sponsor of Get Ahead and personally sent us a cheque each year. It was gestures like this that motivated us to keep going.

What I forgot to mention in my first letter to Jane was how he had deliberately ordered the Anglo American group to start breaking the law; just as we had done. This was in relation to their properties and where we had been acting as nominees for so many black people who had become tenants of the Anglo American buildings. I remedied the situation later.

I later attended the funeral of Peter Magano, my friend and one of the founding members of Get Ahead. It was a happy affair. Everyone was singing. Even President Nelson Mandela flew by helicopter to the town of Ga-Rankuwa, north of Pretoria. He got into the swing of things and said that he, the president, was absolutely confident that Peter Magano had started his work up in heaven straight away by already forming committees for the ANC. It brought the house down—such was the humour of the man.

In the mid-1980s, funerals in black townships assumed a very different added component. They were becoming heavily politicised, and with good reason.

Many of those we were burying had died as a result of police brutality. They had been shot or they had died in detention. The police and government weaponry to dispose of people was enormously powerful. They had the legislation to place people under house arrest, or detain people without trial, or worse. Various states of emergency had been declared, particularly each year around 16 June—the commemorative date for the Soweto student uprisings in 1976.

If a person had died as a result of police brutality, there would definitely be attendance by well-known black political leaders, and quite often, white politicians also attended.

These black politicians would have the opportunity to say a few words and pay tribute: even though they had never met the deceased. One did not have to know the deceased. According to African custom, one does not necessarily have to have known the deceased to be a speaker at their funeral.

It was not always necessary for a politician to speak and often, members of the family or close friends were so bereft that they led forth outbursts against the government.

The funeral proceedings in the main hall would then be followed by the procession to the cemetery where the deceased will be buried. Normally, this is a motorcade with a procession of cars, taxis and buses.

For the political funerals, there was an added dimension. Young men would jog in front of and at each side of the hearse carrying the body of the deceased, chanting and singing as they jogged along. They certainly helped to hype up the event.

Emotions ran high with the mass outpouring from mourners. There would be a public outcry, not only of their anguish but also of their open hostility to the government and police.

As these political funerals became a more regular occurrence, so grew the number of attendees. Thousands of people would come. Funerals would be held on a Saturday morning to ensure that as many people could come as possible.

The problem was exacerbated by the police who, in an attempt to try and quell the anger or feelings of the people, would demonstrate their presence. They would be visible on the tops of security vehicles or buildings. This only angered the people even more.

Occasionally there would be an open confrontation at the funeral between some of the mourners and the police. Tragically, this could lead to an even greater loss of life and meant yet another funeral the next Saturday. It became a vicious cycle, with a political funeral almost each week.

Heart-breaking was that children were also being killed. Jogging next to the hearse, inflamed and incensed, they would torment the police. The police retaliated. And so, there would be yet another funeral.

The security police then decided to impose a rule. At any funeral, there could only be 200 mourners. Anything over and above this would mean that the police would chase away the rest.

This was a hopeless scenario.

As chairman of Lawyers for Human Rights, I was asked to meet with the Special Branch on behalf of the families of people whose funerals would be taking place that weekend. I was introduced to Brigadier Gilles van de Wall. I had seen him before: but not in his police uniform. He was a big rugby forward. He towered above me. He was a lock for the Northern Transvaal rugby team who were then national champions.

I am reasonably short, so this man stood above me like a giant. We sat opposite each other at his desk at the police headquarters.

I made two points in my presentation. The first was that as long as the police continued to show a presence at these funerals, even though they may have the best intentions in the world in attempting to keep law and order, this was not seen by the community in that same light. Rather, it was seen to be confrontational. It was a match that could ignite the funeral into a massive political explosion. Van de Wall said that he would take this matter up with his superiors.

I also raised the issue of the limitation of numbers to 200 mourners. I asked him whether on the death of his father, for example, he would be happy to limit the number of people to 200. Would he be happy if members of the public stood there and counted the people one by one? Surely, his own father deserved better treatment. Could it be better if the police could shield themselves and be in the next street, if needed? They could then be on the spot quickly.

I must have struck a chord because, rather strangely, I noticed that his hand and not mine was shaking. Here was a man gripped with fear—exactly as I had been subjected to, often.

It was by focusing him on a very relevant family issue that I was able to try and persuade him to agree to our request about the limitation of numbers, and the police being out of view. Had I been confrontational and argumentative in my typical anti-government fashion, I don't think I would have got anywhere.

In return, I had to give certain undertakings on behalf of the family. This was not going to be a one-way street. I had to assure him that there would be no running and chanting next to the hearse. We would revert to the orderly vehicle procession. Once at the gravesite, people could then sing and chant and dance and do whatever they want to do. That was different.

The families reluctantly agreed to this condition. We had over 5 000 people at a funeral that following weekend. It went off peacefully.

I reflected on Van de Wall and his shaking hand. He, like me, must have been very nervous about the whole situation. Had there been a blow-up at the funeral he would have been held responsible. Had there been the loss of another life, there would have been a repeat, a week later, of yet another funeral and so the cycle would continue.

His shaking hand certainly led me to realise that there were weaknesses— one just had to find the key.

17 ~ John Vorster Square

The name John Vorster sent cold shivers through many people.

The man himself was a tough archconservative. It was during his time as Minister of Justice that so many repugnant pieces of legislation were passed. These were the legislative enactments that could detain people without trial; keep them in jail for 90 days or longer; confine them to their homes and prohibit them from attending public meetings.

Because of his recognised conservative political strength, he was later to become the leader of the National Party and Prime Minister of the country. It was during this time that many sad events happened. One, for example, was the detention and death of Steve Biko.

I had not heard of Steve until his death in 1967 triggered such a national outcry from Pan Africanists and black leaders, as well as the world, that we very soon got to know who he was. We also realised that the black consciousness movement was a force to be reckoned with.

The name John Vorster also had significant connotations for the police. It was the name of the Central Police Station in Johannesburg, John Vorster Square.

John Vorster Square not only housed ordinary, everyday policemen; it was also the home of the security police. People knew that this was where the Special Branch would torture detainees. Hugh Lewin's book *Bandiet*, among so many others, confirms this.

With the State's security operations directed from John Vorster Square, we heard dreadful accounts of police brutality and transgressions. The apartheid government would embark on cross-border activities into countries such as Botswana, Mozambique and Zambia. We heard reports that Albie Sachs, later to be a Constitutional Court judge, had lost an eye through a letter bomb. Similarly, Ruth First, the wife of struggle leader Joe Slovo, was killed upon receipt of a letter bomb when they were in exile in Mozambique.

There was also mention of how the security machinery somehow engineered a series of events so that the aircraft carrying President of Mozambique, Samora Machel never landed at Maputo International Airport and instead, crashed in South Africa, metres from the Mozambican border, where he sadly died.

Get Ahead gradually built up its own little cache of activities that were illegal in terms of the then-prevailing legislation.

One day, I approached our board of directors in Soweto and suggested to them that it was totally wrong and improper and particularly immoral for black traders not to be allowed to lease business premises in downtown Johannesburg, or Pretoria, or other white cities. I suggested that I would act as the tenant in any building, sign the lease but then more specifically, have a separate agreement with the actual trader who would assume full responsibility in terms of the lease agreement. This meant that the trader would become the de facto lessee. As such, the trader would have to take over all the responsibilities which flowed from the lease agreement. These would include paying the rent, maintaining the property, and keeping it neat.

One also had to have a benign landlord, and this is where I saw how money talks! Most downtown Johannesburg landlords were soon more than willing to use our services as tenants to let their shops and offices to genuine traders.

I remember Bishop Tutu holding a coin in his hand, pointing at it, and saying: "This rand coin is the same for all of us. It buys a loaf of bread; or a cold drink. It does not have a black face on one side and a white face on the other."

Encouraged by this, our board resolved that we would help all black traders who wished to trade on the main street. We embarked on what was to become a very big business for us. We even hired a lawyer, Lindiwe Mtimkulu, to handle all the transactions and were able to help people who wished to start up hair salons, takeaway stores, cobblers and seamstresses— we were amazed at how many people we were able to help, even doctors and lawyers.

It was an utterly crazy law—people were denied economic access. They were denied economic opportunity because of the colour of their skin. They could not operate in their area of first choice, or in the area where the preferred and obvious market was situated.

The law was such that they had to operate in the black townships; places like Soweto and Mamelodi.

I am sure that we attracted the attention of the security police because of our acting as nominees for people. We started off small, but soon word got around and we became highly sought-after. So many people who wanted to trade on the main street got in touch with us. It was they who secured the lease with the landlord; all we did was merely put our names down as signatories to the lease agreements.

One person who was excited about this illegal activity was Ambassador Ed Perkins, who was the USA ambassador to South Africa at the time. Ed was a special person who had a deep concern for the disadvantaged. Bill Swing was another such USA ambassador. He spent many hours with us in the townships and was wonderfully supportive in whatever our initiatives were.

Ed Perkins had another thing going for him.

He was the first black ambassador appointed by the US government to South Africa. Obviously, it was meant to carry a symbolic statement to our government.

We often used to take tours to the townships. We took potential donors and other really interested people. For white South Africans, most of them had never been to a township. For overseas visitors, ambassadors, fund givers and the like, it was a very novel experience.

When I first met Ed, it was in his office and I invited him to take a tour of what we were doing. This was all useful for us because we could then invite other US companies who might wish to become donors. Jenny Williams used to organise these tours at least once a month. We would hire a small bus, or sometimes a big bus, depending on the number of people involved.

When I suggested to Ed that he come on our tour, I also happened to let slip that we acted as nominees for black people who wished to trade down on the main street. He immediately responded by saying that this interested him more. He would rather do a tour of our black businesspeople for whom we were acting as nominees.

So, our first tour with Ed was just that: it was a tour of black businesses doing business in downtown Pretoria. He thoroughly enjoyed that trip!

A few weeks later, he joined us on one of our regular monthly bus tour trips around Mamelodi, where we would show potential donors the small businesses we had helped start in the township. This was to encourage them to support us.

We were rather surprised when, on our way out of the township, our bus was pulled off to the side of the road and armed policemen came on board and asked what we had been doing in Mamelodi. We explained that we were there to look at some of the small businesses which we had started. They asked what all these other people were doing there. We explained that these were people who had given us money or who might give us money to support the small businesses.

It is a little embarrassing, to put it mildly, when you have an international guest, someone whom you were trying to woo for money, only to have the security police stop your vehicle, climb on board heavily armed and start asking you questions. However, this rather confrontational approach may even have helped our fundraising cause!

We then started receiving slightly different requests that would have quite a significant impact on the course of events that were to follow.

Some of our black friends said that they would now like to start moving out of Soweto. They would like to live in a normal white suburban area. Could we help?

Our attitude was that if we were helping people to be tenants in buildings to run their businesses; it was not such a big step forward to enable people to own land in downtown Johannesburg or Pretoria. So, we agreed.

This was when the security police called.

I was invited to meet Detective Sergeant Visagie on the 2nd floor of the John Vorster Square building in Johannesburg. Mindful of what events had occurred at John Vorster Square, I was rather anxious, to put it mildly. One was aware of the fact that certain political prisoners allegedly 'threw' themselves out of the window of the 6th floor only to die. These were made to look like suicides.

I was driven to John Vorster Square by Joe Ramangoa. I was fairly confident that I could handle myself in the interview process.

Just to be on the safe side, as a precautionary measure, I said to Joe, "If I am not back in an hour, this is the telephone number of Helen Suzman. This is the telephone number of the *Sunday Times*, the largest circulating newspaper. Here is the name of the editor. Tell them where I am."

I will say this of Detective Sergeant Visagie: he was more than helpful. He was not the typical bully-type police officer. He was not the sort of person that I had in mind for a security policeman.

He asked me whether I was acting as nominee for the owner of a particular house in a Johannesburg suburb. He gave me the street number. He gave me the name of the occupant. I confirmed that I was helping that person.

"You realise that you are breaking the law," he said.

I responded honestly and openly, saying that I did but for good reasons. One of the reasons is for the economic advancement of people. I then asked Detective Sergeant Visagie if he owned the ground on which his house stands.

"Yes," he replied.

That is all that I am asking for our people, I told him. Again, I asked him if he was denying black people the right to own a house over their heads for themselves and their families, when he already has one.

He then backtracked in an almost apologetic way saying: "Look, I did not make the law. But I have to enforce it."

I gathered from this conversation that Detective Sergeant Visagie might not have been all that convinced of the merits or morals of what he was having to do.

"Are you Donald L. MacRobert?" he asked me

I confirmed my identity.

I asked him how many people he had in this particular division. He told me that there were six policemen tasked with the duty of the surveillance of Groups Areas Act infringements. It was they who would investigate cases of such breaches then lay a charge against both the nominee, which could have been me, or the rightful owner. There were prosecutions brought under the Act, and people who were found guilty were evicted once convicted.

This was the start of quite a long and interesting relationship with Detective Sergeant Visagie of the security police.

I was out well within the hour to meet Joe, who was waiting in the car.

Only six policemen to patrol or check on the whole country, I mused, as Joe and I drove back to the office. They may well be on top now, but things could change.

At the next social justice meeting of AMCHAM, I suggested that we at Get Ahead, together with AMCHAM organise a meeting to which we would invite all the real estate agents in Johannesburg. We would tell them what we were doing in the form of acting as nominees for blacks to own property.

We would encourage them to start following this example. We would tell them that there would be a lot more clients in the pipeline. They could do a lot more business.

We knew that the fear factor would drive away quite a few potential real estate agents. However, some might be quick enough to see the huge potential gap.

Some did.

We started in a small way. Soon the numbers grew.

My arrangement with all these new property owners was the same. I was merely a facilitator. Should they sell the property and realise a profit, the entire profit would be theirs—I did not take a cent of commission.

On the other side of the coin, the obligations and responsibilities that went with property ownership were all theirs. I had no obligations. They had to make sure that they repaid the mortgage bond repayments; the land property rates and taxes; and water and lights accounts.

It is truly remarkable that even though, by law, I would have been held responsible for any negligence or failure on the part of the borrowers, there was only one case out of many hundreds which let me down. A guy failed to tell me that he had reneged on his mortgage bond repayments, but more importantly that the bank was repossessing the property and had issued a summons which they nailed to the front door. This was to cause some hassles later on.

A short while after this big meeting of the Johannesburg real estate agents, we were now doing quite good business. We were acting as nominees for a number of people. They were all moving into the white suburbs. It was actually quite exciting.

I happened to mention this to Helen Suzman in late 1986 that if I was then charged, prosecuted and convicted for all the houses where I was acting as a nominee, I would have up to 1 000 years of jail facing me.

Laughingly, she said that the State would make it easy. They would make all my jail sentences run concurrently and I was probably facing a 20-year jail sentence—at the most.

Just then, Detective Sergeant Visagie from the security police phoned. He said that we needed to meet. My heart sank: I did not feel like going back to John Vorster Square again, especially now that we were becoming bigger players on the block as far as our property ownership was concerned.

I was pleasantly surprised when he said that he would come and visit me—
he came all the way from Johannesburg to visit me at our offices in Pretoria.
He arrived with quite a few sheets of paper and started verifying against our
records, which were the properties where we were acting as nominees. We
seemed to be by far the major property holder on his books.

This time, Detective Sergeant Visagie did not admonish me. He did not
threaten me with any legal action. He merely came to check on our records
and to verify these against his.

We had a good chat over a cup of coffee. We spoke about non-contentious
topics and when he had finished his coffee, he left.

Under slightly awkward circumstances struck up a remarkable friendship,
and after that, he would telephone me and say: "Donald, is stand number
423 in Mondeor yours?" I would phone him back a bit later on to confirm.

And that was then the start of a new verification arrangement. We would do
these by telephone and he would always start off by saying: "Donald L."
because all the properties were being registered in my name.

This created havoc for PricewaterhouseCoopers. Chris Dey, a long-standing
friend and senior partner of the firm has always looked after my personal
affairs.

In fact, he had very little to do once we started Get Ahead because I had no
income. For three years there was no income whatsoever. He always does
things so professionally, precisely.

I was starting to give him headaches.

At a subsequent meeting of real estate agents where we continued to
promote our activities of acting as nominees, one of the people present
worked out that my annual mortgage bond repayments amounted to $10
million per annum. I looked like I was a very rich guy!

But this, of course, causes a professional accountant a lot of headaches.

By law, I was the true owner of those properties, even though the various individuals for whom we were acting as nominees were the borrowers, and it was they who were making the mortgage bond repayments.

We often heard stories about one person or business keeping different sets of accounts. There was the first set of accounts for the bank manager to keep him happy. Then there was another set of accounts for the Receiver of Revenue, the authority where taxes are paid. And then there was the true set.

We decided that it would be necessary to move all my assets off balance sheet. We simply kept a separate record of the various transactions. Indeed, we had filing cabinets full of these property transactions in the end.

We soon moved to holding properties in other centres: Pretoria; Cape Town and Durban.

Detective Sergeant Visagie phoned me to say that he and his five members of staff could no longer cope. Events had overtaken them. They could no longer check on all these property deals, let alone bring the people to court and prosecute them for contravening the law.

Not so long ago, I was in touch with Constitutional Court Judge Sisi Khampepe. While she was still a junior advocate, we plotted to get her a new house in white Johannesburg. We laughed when we remembered the bundles of laws blocking the way. Still, I felt sorry for Detective Sergeant Visagie; he was a good man and did his part to play an important role in advancing black people under South Africa's apartheid regime.

18 ~ Civil Disobedience

Get Ahead Foundation started very slowly.

We had packaged it right, but it had not yet taken off quite the way we wanted to.

Then, eventually, we received our first big grant, which came from the Bishop's World Relief Fund via the Episcopal Church in 2nd Avenue, New York. This enabled us to lend out more money. More particularly, we could start putting together success stories.

We could show them how previously unemployed people had now started their own businesses and they were starting to employ others, creating jobs.

We could show photographs.

We prepared small brochures.

Then a good friend, Simon Steward who was at that stage the South African representative for Chase Manhattan Bank, got interested. Simon has always had his heart in the right place. He had a good career moving up the economic ladder and now, he was looking after Chase in South Africa.

But Chase, along with so many of the other American companies, was under pressure.

Reverend Leon Sullivan had announced his code. American companies who were doing business in South Africa had to comply with the Sullivan Principles and it meant that they had to give a certain percentage of their payroll—and it was a high percentage—to specific causes such as education, health and housing, to uplift the previously disadvantaged. Their employees also had to spend time participating in community service projects.

But the one area where the USA companies were falling short was in job creation.

Simon had become chairman of the task force for AMCHAM and the Sullivan Signature Group responsible for the set of principles of the code.

He persuaded his committee that they should endorse Get Ahead. This endorsement was wonderful because it meant that most of the US companies would give money to Get Ahead. And they did, extremely generously so. I still cast my mind back and think of the huge amounts of money which we received overall from the USA companies. People like Citicorp, Caterpillar, Coca-Cola, Borden, John Deere, Oral B, DuPont—I mention a few but there were many others as well. We were extremely grateful to them (I attach a list of donors as Annexure 1, as prepared by Wendy Richards in 1996).

Then Reverend Sullivan turned up the heat. He felt that not enough was being done in the way of actual protests against the government.

I happened to mention to some of the AMCHAM members that we might be able to play a role because of the humanitarian work which we were doing such as building illegal clinics, or acting as nominees for black businesses who wished to trade on the main streets.

I was surprised one day when people from a place known as Mathibe Stad arrived at our office and appealed to us for help. We asked what we could do?

They asked us to build them a clinic! A very tall order.

Which is virtually what we did. We had the plans drawn by Ora Joubert, a close friend and an architect who worked for and with us. She had obtained her architect degree cum laude from the University of Pretoria where her father was the Rector. She was extremely empathetic to the cause. The building went up. The medical equipment installed. Nursing staff were engaged. We had our clinic – with no permission obtained. Nor was there any interference from any official.

Then came the important question: How would we finance the clinic?

We were able to persuade the Upjohn Foundation of Kalamazoo, USA to part with $50 000. The US dollar went a long way in our country when building projects such as these.

We were delighted the approval came through from Kalamazoo.

So, without obtaining any official permission, we went ahead and completed building the clinic.

The community was excited, and they all helped to mix cement; or collect stones nor sand whenever needed.

Then some strange things happened.

Firstly, we received a letter from the government Department of Health. They enquired whether we were busy building a clinic at Mathibe Stad.

We replied affirmatively. However, we fully believed they would tell us to stop because we did not have official approval; more specifically because the people of Mathibe Stad were being forced to move.

On the contrary. They told us that once the building had been completed and the clinic was ready that they would like to pay for the monthly salary of the nursing sisters who would work there. This came as a complete surprise.

It was very welcome news.

There is a wonderful tradition in Africa when you want to celebrate something. You celebrate by roasting an ox and you invite everybody in to join in the festival and the eating of the meat and drinking of cold drink or beer to celebrate the occasion.

As the clinic neared completion, a date was set, and the necessary preparations were put in hand. An ox was chosen. The necessary catering arrangements were concluded. Plates, knives and forks were borrowed.

The big day arrived, and unlike western events, this is a long affair. It can go on all afternoon; or even all day.

There was a great air of excitement and expectation because friends from the Upjohn company would be officially opening the clinic.

Imagine our surprise when the government officials from various departments also arrived. We were puzzled. Had they come to stop us? Would they close the clinic? Could we go ahead with the official opening?

Rather surprisingly, they told us that they had come to join in the festivities. They were pleased with the fact that the clinic had been built.

We were astounded. In effect, they were condoning what we had done.

We were asked to join the American Chamber's Social Justice Committee. This was chaired by Marius Furst from Hewlett-Packard, with other members such as Ian Leach from Caterpillar, Peter Ritches at IBM, Willem Dercksen from Borden, Roger Crawford from Johnson & Johnson, and of course, Simon Steward from Chase Bank.

Jenny Williams, our star fundraiser at Get Ahead, and I, were the only members of this AMCHAM subcommittee who did not actually work for a US-owned company. We were the outsiders.

Our presence was intended to add a bit of spark to the proceedings.

American companies were under tremendous pressure, South Africa was a bad news item. Headlines in newspapers constantly had stories about the terrible National Party regime; what it was doing either in the form of new legislation, or police action, or brutal cabinet statements and actions.

On top of this, Reverend Sullivan and the Sullivan Principles made the lives of executives of US companies in South Africa absolute hell. Rather than devote all the time to production, marketing, sales and bottom-line profits; suddenly managing directors and CEOs were running around Soweto opening creches; cutting ribbons; kissing babies; and attending black-organised functions. Their time was stretched far beyond what was normally required of an ordinary businessperson.

On top of this, they were subjected to constant pressure from head office back in the USA. Head office would complain that the local company was not doing enough.

Each year, US companies were rated by the Arthur D. Little group in Boston. Those who performed well were given an 'A' rating. Those who performed badly were given a 'C' rating. There could be movement between the As; Bs and Cs, depending on how one performed each year.

A poor performance resulting in a C rating would mean certain punitive measures could take place in the USA. Thus, one might lose certain state contracts in the USA where one was supplying goods to the state; or for municipal contracts.

The local CEO was also subjected to constant visits by head office in the USA. The vice president would arrive then the president, and sometimes, the chairman.

Each time the CEO had to drop his normal work, such as it then was, and take the visiting dignitary on a round of meetings with black leaders, church leaders, community leaders. Coupled with a whole host of visiting projects, they had to be more public in that the local subsidiaries of US companies had to be more outspoken or vociferous in their criticism of the government.

Having sat in on various meetings of the Social Justice Committee, I tentatively suggested that one could investigate the possibility of certain actions which, in effect, would amount to civil disobedience. The USA companies serving on the committee said that they could never support such actions—they merely wanted the investigation undertaken.

So, Jenny and I, along with Peter Magano, Djundju Mathibe and some of our other Robben Island Old Boys created a think tank. We spent a morning discussing what citizens could do in protest. We also thought of what companies could do.

We put down our thoughts on paper. Pam Taylor, who had been with us for a long time, typed up the memorandum. It was titled 'Civil Disobedience'.

We handed it out to the AMCHAM Social Justice Committee in May of 1986. Marius Furst, the chairman, said that all parties would take the document and study it. There was never any suggestion at that main meeting that the companies would embark on civil disobedience actions. They made it quite clear that they had to obey the law.

Then the document was leaked.

On 13 June 1986, three days before the tenth anniversary of the 16 June student uprising in Soweto, the *Citizen* newspaper carried a huge front-page article with a banner headline: "Black organisation proposes civil disobedience."

Somebody from that AMCHAM committee obviously felt very uncomfortable. That somebody must have released it to the right-wing *Citizen* newspaper.

The article castigated Get Ahead. How could Get Ahead make such irresponsible proposals by recommending that laws be broken? The article went on to say that members of the board of Get Ahead included Dr Motlana, the political activist, founder of the Soweto Civic Association and the Soweto Committee of 10. Other board members included Bishop Tutu; renowned for his outspoken criticism of the government.

Another was Tubs Mathabathe, who, 10 years earlier, led the students of Soweto in the uprising.

We were branded as the bad guys, actively going around promoting the breaking of the law.

The *Citizen* newspaper raged on for days about us. There were editorials, op-eds and so on.

On 14 June, the security police hit us. Hard.

At 3:00pm in the afternoon, they raided all seven of our offices at exactly the same time.

Imagine the shock of Nelson Phiri, a shy young man who was looking after our Soweto office, when the door suddenly burst open that afternoon and 10 heavily armed policemen carrying rifles burst in, and immediately demanded to search the premises.

They turned the place upside-down.

They were looking for any document which could implicate anyone politically.

They found nothing at our Soweto office. There were only files regarding loans to clients; and business training classes for them.

For Nelson, it was a shattering experience.

I was not at our head office in Pretoria when the Special Branch arrived— I had been out fundraising with Jenny and we arrived about five minutes after them. We saw cars with huge aerials waving in the air. There were police vans with blue lights flashing. They had blocked off the road.

We parked our car and gingerly walked into our office.

I introduced myself. The chief security policeman, Superintendent Detective Blaauw—I will never forget his name—introduced himself to me. He told me that they were looking for anti-government documents.

I told them to look around and help themselves.

I telephoned Marianne and told her what had happened.

She galloped to the office and was soon with us.

Most of the staff tried to carry on with their normal duties while 10 security police, men and women, opened filing cabinets and drawers, and checked each desk for anything incriminating.

What appealed to them most, and they pounced on it, was any letter to or from Archbishop Tutu. Similarly, any letter to our chairman Dr Motlana, or from him, was eagerly snatched.

These were harmless letters. Most of them dealt with the day-to-day administration of the company; loans, finances, business training courses and the like. Yet, because of the personalities involved, they were eagerly grabbed.

I then realised the hatred that people had for some of our board members. If they could find anything that might, in any way, have implicated our board members, being black political opponents of the government, then this would be good meat!

After the security police had been with us for about an hour, and were busy going through every cupboard, shelf and filing cabinet, I said to Marianne: "Why don't you offer them some coffee?"

Her reply, and I will never forget it: "Not a damn. They can go to hell."

Remember: our telephones were already being tapped and our mail intercepted. Soon afterwards, my immediate brave outer posture seemed to crack a bit, and I felt that my hands were just about to start shaking.

I immediately started photocopying. I photocopied anything to keep my hands and myself busy.

I got hold of the book by Reverend Sullivan, which had been given to me by Bishop Richard Kraft. Titled *Build, Brother, Build*, it describes how Reverend Sullivan himself had started offering training courses to people in the ghettos of Philadelphia. He had called his centre, O.I.C., which also had a phonetic ring of "Oh, I see."

Although the copies were not required at all, I busied myself all afternoon making photocopies.

The Special Branch were back at our head office the next day. This time they were more intent in what they were looking for.

They had procured a copy of the Civil Disobedience memorandum that I had authored after the discussions with my colleagues and friends at Get Ahead—the same copy that formed the basis of the screaming headlines on the front page of the *Citizen* newspaper on June 13, 1986.

Superintendent Detective Blaauw wanted to know where the document had been typed. They investigated all the typewriter machines, computers and printers in our office. Eventually, they found Pam Taylor's typewriter. It seemed to match. They took away the typewriter.

They also took away with them all the letters to and from Bishop Tutu and Dr Motlana. We were given a receipt for the documents and typewriter. We never saw these documents or the typewriter until after Nelson Mandela became president of our country eight years later, in 1994.

This experience led me to introduce a useful but interesting clause in our contracts of employment with our staff. The staff were granted leave. This could be holiday leave, sick leave or study leave. We realised that the security forces of the State may do certain things to certain family members which would automatically result in our members having to absent themselves from work. We then introduced a heading for compassionate leave because we had no control over these matters and had a moral obligation to make the necessary allowances.

We went even further to introduce a detention clause in our employment contracts. This clause stated that if anyone was detained or imprisoned by the police it was incumbent on us to continue paying that person's salary to ensure groceries, food and other provisions were available to the family for the duration of that person's detention. This clause was only invoked once, when Peter Magano was jailed by the security police.

The raids on 13 June simultaneously launched on all seven of our offices had an interesting twist in Mamelodi.

At the time, Philemon Machene managed the office. It is a small office on the ground floor of an office block. Philemon used to run his business by sitting behind his desk and customers who were waiting for loans would sit on a bench, in the same room, opposite him. He had about five people sitting on the bench waiting for their loans to be processed. He would deal with them all, one by one, taking down their details. Philemon then happened to look up and glance out the window. He saw armed security forces swarming over the roof towards the office.

Philemon immediately vacated his seat, ran around the desk and sat on the bench alongside the other waiting customers and when the door burst open followed by 10 security police, there was no one sitting in the official chair.

The leader barked: "Where is the organiser?"

"He's gone to town and will only be back tomorrow," Philemon politely replied.

The security police left, empty-handed and disappointed.

GOING UP — AND DOWN

PA News — 15/6/74

SIR,—There was muttering in the basement,
grumbling on the stairs;
the building was unhappy
with the state of affairs.

The problem concerned the lifts
and the signs above each door,
reading "Whites," "Bantu," "Service" —
varying from floor to floor.

The routes are clear on ground floor,
but the higher one ascends
the signs are less apparent —
and even absent on the tenth.

Now a messenger came to visit
and entered the right plek,
proceeded to the tenth,
but left by a different hek.

The matter was reported
and the caretaker to be sure
searched all over for the rascal
who, alas, was found no more.

So the moral of the story —
and the lifts with all their jerking —
is: irrespective of one's colour
they always keep on working.

— DON McROBERT.
Pretoria.

As far back as 1960s, Don was writing letters to the *Pretoria News* drawing
attention to the apartheid system, and he did it in verse form. This letter, dated
15 June 1974, was about a messenger entering a building who didn't know which
lift, or elevator, to take; whether there was one for white or black?

19 ~ Sifiso Ngcobo

Sifiso Ngcobo told his mother that he wanted to pass his matric exams and go into the business world. His mother, a widow, supported him as far as she could on her meagre salary.

Sifiso and his mother lived in the heart of Soweto in a suburb called Jabavu, also known as White City. Here, the standard matchbox houses were smaller than in other parts of the township—somehow, the government managed to pack even more people into that very cramped and crowded area.

The problem with this overcrowding was that crime was rife. White City was not the place to be walking around in the dark at night and gangs used to roam the streets, accosting passers-by.

Sifiso did not mind too much as he was able to work and study at home at night. He passed his final matric exams but then came the issue of not being able to enrol at a university. The problem was twofold: the first challenge was money, as his mother could not afford university fees; and the second was that black people could not enrol at the universities or trade schools.

Fortunately for Sifiso, he was able to get a job making fibreglass products, like shelters to cover frames for outside gazebos, canopies for small vans, and especially, repairing dented cars. With such limited access to any economic opportunities, Soweto had very few cars, and its drivers were not known for their skills. Many were self-taught or very new to driving, having learned the basics from someone else, and so there was a growing demand for the services Sifiso could provide.

Sifiso decided to start his own business right in the middle of White City, Soweto. The problem was that there were no factory or business sites available, so he arranged with his mother that he could start making his products right outside her house on the pavement. If ever you go to China, there are hordes of small businesses making and repairing things on the pavement. You can see people repairing bicycles; others have treadle sewing machines; at one stage, part of the road to Xian was used to dry rice, with passing traffic only able to use the remaining side of the road.

At the end of each day, Sifiso couldn't leave his products and raw materials on the pavement, and he agreed with his mother that he would store everything on the roof of her house. In the early mornings on their way to work, people could see a fair bit of activity coming from the roof of this little house.

Sifiso needed money to expand his business and he came to discuss this with us at Get Ahead, where he knew that we loaned small amounts to the upcoming businesspeople. It was clearly stated to Sifiso that he had to repay his loan promptly. Any delay in repayment would result in the cancellation of the loan but on the other hand, if he paid on time or even earlier, he stood to gain by being able to receive a further and bigger loan to help him expand.

It was really tough to be a black person in those days. They were described by former Prime Minister Verwoerd, as being "hewers of wood and drawers of water". That was their lot; consigned to the bottom of the heap.

Under the apartheid regime, a black person could not own land or a house. This meant they could never borrow from the banks and use their house as collateral to secure a loan that could enable them to start a new business, or pay student fees and loans.

Hernando de Soto from Peru chastised his government for not granting loans to the poor. He proposed that in squatter camps, people could be allocated small land parcels in their name, which could be used as security for a bank loan. He did wonderful work for the poor, providing the sort of assistance that Sifiso needed so badly but the legal mountain of apartheid laws that were stacked against him were dreadful.

Apart from these laws, there were practices that blocked the way for emerging black entrepreneurs.

142

I was surprised when, one day, long before the advent of cell phones, my desk telephone rang. The caller said: "Morning Don. Do you have some time to explain some of the laws and practices to me?"

I nearly fell off my chair. Here was Derek Keys, the then Minister of Finance of our South African cabinet calling me on his own, not using a secretary or switchboard operator to call. No! He was calling by himself.

As luck would have it, I had the information at my fingertips, as I had tried to respond earlier to a rather grumpy newspaperman on the same subject.

I was able to explain to the Minister that black people were never granted loans by the banks then—for whatever purpose, for a car, student fees, or a home. The laws also prohibited them from owning businesses in downtown white areas and prevented them from being skilled workers. Mining laws, as an example, reserving certain jobs for whites only. No train driver could be black. They could not buy shares in companies. The stock exchange was a no-go. Blacks were designated to be lackeys; underpaid and unskilled. Trade schools for blacks did not exist and they were barred from universities.

His friendly and courteous manner arose from a previous meeting when he had kindly invited me to join his prayer group early each Monday morning. He was a big businessman who was then the chairman of many listed companies but living in Pretoria, I unfortunately could not accept his kind offer of a Monday meeting in Johannesburg.

From red tape and endless forms, to long queues for blacks, the challenges explained to the Minister were some of the obstacles facing Sifiso and many others wanting to start their own businesses.

At this stage, Wendy Richards and I were able to take a friend from Australia, Gilbert Shearer, on a trip to visit Sifiso. More particularly, Gilbert had two other Australian friends, Norbert Byrne and John Connolly with him. Norbert and John were members of the International Rugby Board. They had brought two other board members, and the six of us had coffee and sandwiches standing on the pavement outside Sifiso's mother's house. The international visitors were amazed at his factory with all his raw materials on the roof. Of course, they were not all that interested in his fibreglass products, but rather, his manner of working.

I will say this for Minister Derek Keys. Things started to change. One noticed that the bullying and harassment by the police against small traders, like the hawkers, seemed to abate.

Later, legislation made it possible for blacks to own property.

With careful planning, saving, and true grit, Sifiso was eventually able to buy a small piece of land opposite his mother's house, where he started his first proper factory making fibreglass products. He then knocked down the small matchbox house where his mother lived and built her a very neat and pleasing cottage.

Sifiso was not the only person who was helped. There were hundreds of thousands to whom a helping hand was given. Looking over our regular reports and newsletters, we were able to expand from our original activities of granting small loans to the very poor.

Get Ahead's mission started out to empower the informal economic sector of the black community through job creation, by providing micro-enterprise loans. Over time, the activities of the company were expanded to promote the communal and business interests of blacks.

The 1995 newsletter reported on the activities of Get Ahead expanding into a range of areas. This included a microcredit programme where we pioneered the concept of lending money to people in groups to enable them to start their own businesses. It was amazing how many jobs could be created and how many businesses were started at this level.

To further assist small traders, we built informal trading stalls in many of the townships around South Africa. It should be remembered that the black townships only catered for residents and not trading.

Through our business training programme, we offered courses in costing, pricing, marketing, bookkeeping. We also developed a technical skills training component offering welding, panel beating, motor repairs, carpentry, sewing, knitting.

Abetted by Archbishop Tutu and headed by Marina Clark, we also started a primary healthcare wing. This used the so-called 'barefoot doctor' concept, where we trained people to become primary healthcare workers. These so-called *nompilos* followed the WHO training courses.

Get Ahead was eventually able to expand from its hub of Johannesburg and Pretoria to establish offices in Durban, East London, Port Elizabeth, Cape Town and Nelspruit. We were able to enlist the services of people who were able to track the efforts of Get Ahead.

Generally, only 20% of new start-ups make it past two years, with the other 80% having fallen by the way-side. Get Ahead's reports showed the opposite—80% of our small businesses were still in existence after two years of trading. Sometimes the harshness of the climate in the black townships made it imperative to keep trading.

Historical evaluations of Get Ahead show that, in 1997, as an example, the bad-debt write-offs by Get Ahead Financial Services amounted to R130 000 on a total annual loan book of just under R20 million.

About 90% of the borrowers were women. They had the drive to start small businesses to create a money supply to enable them to feed and educate their children. Think of the stories told in this book: people like Mrs Chauke and her sale of *mielies* at the railway station; or Sophie, the shebeen queen, or tavern owner; or Beauty Sithole pulling herself up the ladder from being a cleaner.

I think of so many women who worked hard to pull themselves up the poverty ladder. Daphne Motsepe was such a woman, who lived in Atteridgeville outside Pretoria, but who worked in Johannesburg. She was working for one of the large chartered accountancy firms. Apart from her work by day, she was having to study by night to get through her chartered accountancy examinations.

I remember Daphne saying that because of the apartheid system she could not get any accommodation near her work in Johannesburg. This meant that she would get up at 4:30am in the morning, walk to the Atteridgeville station to catch her first train into downtown Pretoria. She would then change trains and catch another train to Johannesburg. After that, she would catch a bus or a taxi to get her to the office of the chartered accountants. All this to be there by 8:00am. It consisted of a journey of at least two hours every morning.

And then two hours back in the evening. Afterwards, she would have to study for her chartered accountancy examination.

On another occasion we met some school girls living North of Pretoria, who, in their thirst for education, caught a bus to Pretoria then a train out to Mamelodi, followed by a walk to their school. This was a journey of at least one and a half hours each morning and one and half hours for the return journey in the late afternoon or early evening. Can you imagine how tired and exhausted the pupils must have felt every day?

I remember on one occasion before 8.00am at the Get Ahead Office, I saw Ziphora Malaudi sitting at her desk with her head down on her arms. I asked her; "are you feeling ok?" Her response was, "Pa, I'm exhausted because even coming to work we have had the security police stopping the buses and taxis bringing us to work. It puts us under much stress."

Once, in Kenya, Marianne and I saw a notice board saying: "Educate a man, you educate an individual, but if you educate a woman, you educate a whole nation." Too true for me.

Furthermore, I noted that in 1996, Get Ahead created 40 000 jobs in the informal sector.

It is also very pleasing that some traders moved from the informal to the formal sector, like Sifiso, and are still going strong today. They were able to expand their financial wherewithal to buy a house, a motorcar and educate their children well.

Reverse take-over

The Provincial Council opening occurred
Last Tuesday and when much was heard
About roads and youth and teaching too
The Administrator spoke of much to do

Now the gallery was packed with visiting friends
Who'd come to see the new members' trends
They sat on the benches and stood in the aisle
The speeches were long so they waited a while

All the benches were full, excepting for two
Which although quite empty were "Reserved" —
     but for who?
Two gentlemen finding the strain on their feet
Decided there must be one vacant seat

So quietly they moved and plonked themselves down
On one "Reserved" bench which had no one around
The Commissionaire spied them and moved in neat
Saying "You may not sit on this Reserved seat"

"Why not," asked the men — "it's not in use"
The official replied "It's reserved for Bantus"
They left as the message was polite, but terse
How's that for Apartheid in Reverse?
— DON MacROBERT.
Waterkloof.

Here is a poem Don wrote for the *Pretoria News* that ran in the 13 May 1974 edition, where the provincial legislator had special seats in the gallery for blacks on one side, and whites on the other.

20 ~ Tough Woman

After my sojourn in Soweto—about 10 years later when I was back practising law—blacks were still facing many challenges in the townships, where jobs and training facilities, did not exist. Despite this, many overcame the obstacles facing them, with Beauty Sithole being one of them.

Beauty is a woman to whom these four words can be ascribed: driven; determined; warm; mother.

I was working for a patent law firm in Pretoria in the mornings and another firm in Johannesburg in the afternoons. I would leave the first firm at lunchtime, returning later in the evening. After going to gym in the early morning, I would arrive at the Pretoria firm quite early to get the show on the road, often turning on the office lights in the morning. This is where I met Beauty.

She was a cleaning lady who came in early in the morning having travelled from the Mamelodi train station, the same one where Mrs Chauke sold her *mielies*, except Beauty lived quite a distance and had to walk from her home to the station, adding more time to her already long day. She was also a single mother with two young children.

Having arrived at the law firm, she would go to the carpark basement in the building. This had a cloakroom for black ladies. She would take off her clothes and shoes, replacing them with a grey uniform and slippers. Now she was ready to start her duties, cleaning every office, especially the wastepaper basket in each. Lawyers make a meal about all the paper they discard. Being the second or third person to appear on our floor, she would greet me every morning with a friendly smile. She never complained.

One morning she knocked on my door, which was always open, and asked if I could spare a few minutes. She wanted to ask me a question. "Sure," I said.

"Sit down. How can I assist?" I asked.

"I want to learn about typing, and computers," she started. A tall order, I thought, but let's listen...

"I have searched around, and downtown, near the main railway station, there is a secretarial college. I can catch the train from Mamelodi station to town, followed by a short walk. They offer a special course on Saturday and Sunday mornings for beginners who have other jobs during the week. I can learn about computers and their programmes."

I was impressed by Beauty and her drive—she had walked a very difficult road, with significant hurdles along the way. I had to ask: "What about the weekends, and your two young children?"

She had thought about that, she said, and her mother would look after them on Saturdays and her sister offered to help on Sundays.

She was resolute in her determination.

"Why don't we go this Saturday morning, to inspect the place, and find out more about the courses they provide?" I offered.

In the back of my mind, I thought about these fly-by-night operations and their pie-in-the-sky courses; here today, gone tomorrow—a rip-off and total sham.

I met Beauty that Saturday in a building at the top of Bosman Street, near the train station. I was pleasantly surprised—it was a clean place, almost like a smart office. The lady in charge greeted us warmly and started by asking Beauty what she would like to learn or gain from the course. She confidently said that she wanted to learn how to type and about computers, but she admitted to not having any such skills or knowledge and didn't know how a computer worked, or even where to turn it on... I knew the feeling!

The mainstream use of computers in the workplace occurred while I was still working in Soweto. Marianne picked it up quickly, but I had been left far behind after a sorrowful experience when I eventually joined the Johannesburg law firm in 1998. Miranda Feinstein offered to introduce me to Sally Story of ExecuTrain. I didn't do well there. I eventually accepted the shortest course for two people so that I could have the instructor entirely to myself, without any other interfering clever person. Evidently, I am a slow learner.

The lady heading up Beauty's training centre explained that with the country's economy slowly opening up, there were a growing number of secretarial posts for blacks, especially in the country's capital, Pretoria, with its growing civil service corps. She mentioned some of their success stories but I wasn't completely convinced. I suggested that if Beauty attended each weekend class and was showing competence; passing her bi-monthly tests, I would be prepared to pay half of the tuition fees, provided Beauty could pay the rest. That seemed fair to everyone. "Let's see," I mused to myself. But Beauty excelled, and when she showed me her progress reports, I realised that she might already be passing me by! Technology and I are not the most compatible of friends.

During one occasion, when in San Francisco with Marianne, she wanted to telephone at 8.00pm one night, to wish her lovely father in Pretoria a happy birthday. This would mean we would be connected with him at 7.00am in the morning in South Africa. One of our US friends, Ron Lehrman invited us to join them in a restaurant in China Town. We declined, saying that we had better stay at the hotel, so we did not miss speaking to Marianne's father. We needed to wait to be connected by the hotel operator, and that all takes time.

"Such a miserable excuse," said Ron. "This is America—this is the real world! Come to dinner. Book your call to Pretoria, get the hotel to do that. Speak from the restaurant. Get the charge to be debited by the restaurant, to your hotel room," I didn't think that was possible. It certainly wouldn't have been in Soweto. But it worked and Oupa was overjoyed. I never let on that I wasn't the clever tech boffin!

One morning, Beauty knocked on my door. She was still a cleaning lady in her grey uniform and slippers, and she had a problem. She could improve on her training if she were able to practice on a computer after hours. At that stage, it was not possible at the Pretoria law firm, so Beauty started exploring if she might be able to buy a second-hand or obsolete computer.

"But you must see if it can work at the place where the children and I stay," she asked.

The following Sunday afternoon, after her Sunday classes, I followed the directions Beauty had given me to her home in Mamelodi. I arrived at the place she had indicated—she had drawn a map of how to get there.

I stopped, and my jaw dropped.

I was in the middle of a squatter camp, where all the homes were shacks and loosely made out of tin. Tin sheets for the walls. Tin sheets for the flat roof over their heads. No proper streets—only dusty, winding roads and paths. There was definitely no running water in the homes and no electricity for light or cooking. The cold must have crept in between the cracks and been dreadful in winter. Beauty lived here, in this one-room shack, with her children.

In the book written by Daniel James Brown, *The Boys in the Boat*, it tells the story about a group of boys from Seattle who eventually won the gold medal for rowing at the 1936 Olympic Games in Berlin, where Hitler had hoped for a German landslide. Those boys came from very poor backgrounds, with one even wearing the same jersey in his final year at university that he had when worn when he arrived on campus four years before. The book shows a picture of Hooverville, where the boys came from. Described as being a 'shantytown' made up of hundreds of tin shacks, that picture of Hooverville looks exactly the same as that squatter camp did in Mamelodi. Each shack, like Hooverville, consisted of one small room, with leaking walls and roofs. And it never stopped the cold.

"Please come inside," said Beauty. I stepped into her home. Two mattresses were stacked side by side, on top of the bed, to make space. There were two small tables, one of which had a kettle for hot water, and a small cooking ring to prepare food. I asked Beauty about water. There was a tap up the road, she said. She and the children would draw enough water for cooking at night. They would then have enough to wash themselves in the morning and change into clean clothes each day. It was on the second table that she wanted to put the computer. I had to ask about electricity. You need that for your computer.

She smiled. "I am hot-wired," she said. Her neighbours had run an electric lead from the street pole to power the supply to their shacks, allowing them to cook and even watch television on a tiny screen. Beauty boiled water, illegally, for a cup of coffee. "Let me ask Jeremy at the law firm about a computer. He is helpful. He is the CEO," I offered.

Before going to see Jeremy, the next afternoon, I had to call one of Get Ahead's board members in the USA, Maurice Tempelsman. The call was answered by a clever lady, Barbara, who connected us. At the end of the call, Maurice asked if Dr Motlana and I could meet him the following morning for breakfast.

I couldn't believe my ears. "But you're in New York, and I am in Pretoria?" I asked, puzzled.

No, he told me. He was at the airport in Windhoek, Namibia, and would be boarding a flight to Johannesburg that evening. Barbara had switched the call from New York.

"See you for breakfast tomorrow!" he said.

In Soweto, we could never switch telephone calls like Barbara, and I mention this because Beauty was already ahead of my technology wherewithal!

I spoke to Jeremy. He said they were about to discard some of the slightly older computers. Take one. No charge.

I gave it to Beauty, and she had it working that evening.

Beauty aced her training and equipped with a diploma, she applied to the law firm. She was appointed as a fax machine operator then to a role as a secretary and eventually, she worked within the patent renewals department.

She left her shantytown tin room home and bought a house in one of the new suburbs in Mamelodi; a brick house. She then sold the last house and bought another home in a suburb in Pretoria, in a district formerly for whites only.

Her children are grown up—Beauty sent them to university to make sure that they have a good start in life.

Beauty's career path follows those four words: Driven. Determined. Warm. Motivated.

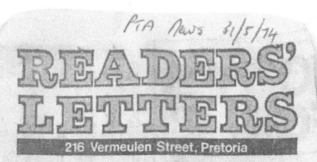

READERS' LETTERS

216 Vermeulen Street, Pretoria

PTA News 31/5/74

Do drop into our parks

SIR, —

If you are a baby in a treetop,
when the bough breaks you'd better stop
to carefully check on the state of your landing —
which may be a park with no proper standing.

Our pilots realise the problem so dear
as right across Africa they're buzzed in the rear.
Around the bulge is the course they are fashioning,
which conflicts with the concept of petrol rationing.

Imagine the quandary facing the birds
migrating southwards in their herds;
they're affected by a colour taboo
with blackbird, yellowbird and redbreast, too.

After miles of travel and feeling grim,
selecting a bough for a weary limb,
is far less acute for a bird who is popping
than to find the right park which accepts his
dropping.

— DON MacROBERT,
Pretoria

Another poem that ran in the *Pretoria News*, 31 May 1974, about what parks a bird makes its droppings in; does it do it in a white or a black park? Difficult to determine from the air!

21 ~ Travel

Going back to that happy evening at Harlequin's bar after spectating the rugby match with Vicky, it was so easy. Relaxed. Enjoyable. That is how it should be when people of different colour meet—they must enjoy themselves and everybody should easily fit in. In this way, we can cover so many topics and issues but very few people questioned the system.

I was somewhat taken aback in Soweto, in the early days there. When you arrived at someone's house, rather than going to the front door and knocking gently, you walk around to the backdoor, from the kitchen. And on the way, you audibly announce yourself so that the lady of the house can easily hear you approaching. I think this is done to be sure that you do not arrive suddenly, giving residents a fright as you appear around the corner. Once heard, you are warmly greeted by the lady of the house.

Djundju and I had arrived at the kitchen door of a potential client, alerting the lady of the house of our arrival. We were welcomed with a friendly smile and greeting. She invited us to come in. I followed Djundju through the door to get into the kitchen. But there was a yell from a young person almost in shock.

"*Umlungu! Umlungu!*" yelled the young boy, of only four years old. "*Umlungu! Umlungu!*" he kept hollering. He hid behind the skirt of his mother. Tears streaming down his face. He was terrified.

The term *umlungu* may be considered by some to be a derogatory word used by blacks to describe a white man. It comes from the Zulu and Xhosa languages.

I pondered about that boy using that word. Living in the deep parts of Soweto, he would not normally see any white people in Soweto, at all. They were barred from entering the area, with big signboards declaring entry was prohibited. So, how did he know about the *umlungu* who appeared at his mother's house? Are we born with inherent prejudices? Does it happen from birth, or is it developed over time—maybe handed down from father to son, or among schoolmates until it is eventually ingrained in us?

He probably did not go to downtown Johannesburg on a Saturday with his mother. He was too young and would likely need to wait a few more years before venturing into the city. Maybe he had seen a white person on the television in the house, or from a family member showing him a book, or a picture. But from his reaction, he had never seen a whitey in the flesh before. His mother apologised effusively. She confirmed that her little boy had not seen living white people before. "Don't worry," I ventured.

But that little boy's fear was there. It was also there with the whites, and from the same origins: fear. We all have it inside, whether we like it, or not, and this is the root of all prejudice.

I wondered about a friend. Let's call him Rodney Mountain. He lives near Cape Town, on a farm. He keeps bees and sells honey to the supermarkets, making a tidy profit from the business. He prays every day and wouldn't ever harm a flea. I bumped into him at another pub, in Cape Town. A place called Forries—an abbreviation from Foresters Arms. At the time, farmers were battling drought, and he said that some of the neighbouring farmers were having a bad time. Business was bad. Couldn't seem to make ends meet. Rodney was telling me that his immediate neighbour needed help on the farm with extra labour. So, Rodney did the honourable thing by sending some of his workforce to help his neighbour. Over a beer, he related the story of how he assisted with the harvest: "Yes, I did the neighbourly thing and sent some of my Afs to help."

Afs. That is another name. An abbreviation for the word 'African'. Said so nicely—no malice at all. For me, this was still tinted with prejudice. Maybe I was surprised at the use of the expression. Not in the least bit offensive to the other white drinkers at the pub. But what about the people who worked for Rodney who might have heard that term used? Surely, they must have reacted in a particular manner? Maybe recoiled. Not saying anything to his face, because the boss is a kind and gentle person who looks after us so well. Is it a throwback from the earlier master-servant relationship, I wondered.

Of course, it wasn't meant that way, at all. On some of the farms, talk is of a much rougher calibre. You might hear white people talking to each other, amongst themselves, using slurs like 'coon'; or 'darkie'. And they bring their language and mannerisms when they drop into the friendly nearby bar at Ramblers in a wheat farming area; or Rawdens where sugarcane is grown.

I must confess that in South Africa, we are not unique. I saw this during happy times we had in a little village in Cambridgeshire, England, in a pub in the country called The Woodman. Its sloping roof meant that the closer you went towards the outside wall, the more you were almost bent double. To balance yourself, you would hold your free hand up against the roof for support and lean against it having a good natter. And of course, the topic got onto the game of cricket, which the English play and enjoy, so passionately. We commented on the play that day, between England and the visiting West Indies team.

"Those West Indies people are good!" one person exclaimed.

"Big blokes!" another chimed in.

"Yes, those darkies have got something," someone added.

"Maybe there is something in the food that they eat?" another patron wondered aloud.

On the surface, it seemed like a regular enough exchange, until you realise this is how people think, speak and behave!

And they are not alone. Swing over the ocean again, to Michigan and some of the motor industry cities. In a bar where we dropped in for a pie, we heard some white workers in their blue overalls discussing "the coons", and even "ni***rs".

They were copycats of South Africa's local motor industry workers, also in overalls, in a pub in Selby, Johannesburg, where the whites would drop in for a quick scotch or two during their lunch break, gulping them down before going back to work. Here, you would hear the same terrible names being used in conversation. I would often think how this sort of mentality of discrimination resulted in the flaring up of gender-based violence—another form of oppression.

This is not confined only to the working class.

It was on a flight from New York to San Francisco when I realised just how unpopular we South Africans were. I was fortunate to have, for some reason, been upgraded to business class on the flight. This was going to be quite pleasant. I would have space to spread my reading material and could sit back and relax from time to time.

Shortly after take-off, a friendly air hostess asked me whether I would like to have coffee or tea. I asked for tea. She offered me a muffin. This was gratefully accepted. She was very polite and courteous.

After having made sure that I was comfortable and that my various needs had been attended to, she commented on my accent. She noted that I was obviously from abroad and asked if I was English. I told her: "No, I am from South Africa," She visibly recoiled. One could see her reaction. She made it quite obvious that she would not be helping me again on that long journey.

I also realised that it would not help my case at all to explain that I was an opponent of the government and its racist policies. It was evident that she would not hear my story if I started telling her that I worked in Soweto to try and help disadvantaged people living there.

Being African-American, she had very definite views on my country and its people, particularly white people. She had immediately classified me as a white supremacist who was trying to keep the black people down.

She must have had words with another of the cabin staff because thereafter, I was looked after by another member of the crew although she, too, was a bit distant.

It certainly became very frosty in the business class cabin of the airplane, whereas I had previously had a group of jovial and happy air hostesses all darting in for the quick hello and how are you. All this vanished into thin air very quickly.

This was a very different experience from a trip a year later to Atlanta. I was allocated an aisle seat. In the seat next to me, the window seat, was an elderly gentleman. He wore a suit and tie. We fell into easy conversation. I learned that he had been a dentist but had retired. He was travelling to see some of his family in the South. I was interested that he had a daughter and granddaughter living near Birmingham, Alabama. They lived far apart and so could not often see each other. There was a high level of excitement.

After we had chatted a while, he asked me where I was from and, bearing in mind my last experience, I was a little bit reticent, but I told him; South Africa. He said: "Oh, you are the people with those racial laws, aren't you?" And I thought, "Here it comes—another explosion!" After my past experience with the airline crew, I wanted to make it clear that I did not support the policies of the government. I had hardly started my protest speech when he interrupted me saying: "Your government is wrong. You are giving away too much to the ni***ers."

Here was a completely opposite viewpoint—I did not expect this at all! Here was a professional man, a dentist, criticising me because our government was doing too much for our black people.

Fortunately, our conversation made him tired. He said that he needed to take a nap, and asked if I would mind.

I gratefully let him go because I was not going to enter into a long political debate with someone who had such firm and rigid views. This would have been a real ding-dong battle, and I was very pleased when he dozed off.

A few months later, I met with a university professor. He had quite a useful working knowledge of South Africa and also knew a fair amount about the US government's policies towards my country. He knew about constructive engagement, the US government's policy of proactively engaging with the South African government with the view of persuading them to change their racist laws. But he felt that there could be more interaction from both sides. The US government agencies needed to become more proactive in dealing with the government agencies in South Africa. Similarly, the South African government should undertake regular visits to the USA to learn from its experiences.

This was all getting a bit too much. I remembered how many years ago one of my black friends had told me that another name for South Africa was Azania. One of the smaller black parties, the PAC, promised that if they came into power, they would change the name of the country to Azania. Very few people knew this at the time, and Azania was hardly ever heard of, let alone known.

Marianne and I decided to adopt a new strategy on our travels. Whenever we encountered people whom we did not know at all, and were most unlikely ever to meet again, and we were asked where we came from, our answer was quite simple: Azania.

The response was usually something like: "Oh, isn't that somewhere out in Africa?" "Yes," we would innocently reply.

The questioner pressed us no further. We were happy. We smiled quietly to ourselves.

These occurrences got me thinking… What makes people tick, or to say things, or act to hurt others? Is it from early on, like that little boy in Soweto, crying as he shouted "*Umlungu!*" to me? Or is it ingrained in how we were brought up?

Maybe we need to think! Then stop! And think, again.

While we have indeed come a long way since the awful days of apartheid, it is clear we still have a fair distance to go, now, before we are able to bring about equal and fair opportunities for all.

We called our efforts 'the struggle' during apartheid era because it took the sheer might and will of many of us to shift perceptions and change our laws to set in motion the wheels of change. My hope is that the will and perceptions will continue to change.

22 ~ Treason Trial

One day, strolling along Church Street in Pretoria, which is its main street, Djundju and I were on our way to the bank to collect some petty cash.

A young man, coming in the opposite direction suddenly embraced me and burst into tears. I did not readily recognise him. Djundju did.

This was Buti Tshabalala, an 18-year-old, who lived in Mamelodi. Standing on the sidewalk, he told us a very sad story.

He told us how the security police had knocked on the door of his family home at 11:00pm the night before. When the door was opened, they rushed and grabbed him. He was not charged with any offence. No formal complaint was levelled at him. He was carted away in an unmarked car, for questioning.

He was brutally manhandled.

He then told us of how he was taken to the security police station in downtown Pretoria. Its name was Compol. To mention it to most blacks and political leaders sent a chill up their spine. This was a chamber of torture and was where people were subjected to interrogation, blindfolding, beatings and many other terrible afflictions.

Buti described to us how he had been interrogated and beaten up at Compol. They had started their interrogation at midnight. He was forced to look into an extremely bright light which started blinding him. Voices questioned him. He gave answers. When they regarded these as being incorrect or insufficient, he was hit and beaten. He showed us how he had lost a tooth. His mouth had been bloodied.

Buti had been beaten around his face. His cheeks bore what were to become big bruises later on. One could see the beginning of the bruises forming. In tears, he described his awful ordeal.

At 7:00am in the morning, the security police realised that despite their beating and battering they were not going to get any more information out of Buti, they cast him out into the streets of downtown Pretoria some 24 kilometres from Mamelodi. They were not even gracious enough to take him back to his home and dump him in Mamelodi. He was turfed out into the streets in downtown Pretoria and expected to walk home to Mamelodi, with no money. This was when he saw us.

I immediately said to Djundju that we should do something for Buti.

Usually, in those circumstances, one would have gone to the police to report the matter. This was an assault charge.

And yet, the last people that I would like to have gone to then would have been the police. It was the Special Branch of the police who had, in fact, perpetrated these violent deeds. I made up my mind immediately not to go to the police.

We went around the corner to the office of the Legal Resources Centre (LRC) founded by Arthur Chaskalson, an eminent lawyer who would become the Chief Justice, under President Nelson Mandela. The Pretoria branch of the LRC was being run and managed by a very good friend, Nick de Villiers, who had become a stalwart lawyer acting for political prisoners. He was also very defiant in his verbal attacks on the security police.

We went to see Nick at the LRC centre. Buti gave a full statement of what had happened. Nick recorded this. He suggested to Buti that it might be possible to sue the Minister of Police and to claim damages. Buti said he would think about this. We then took Buti to the district surgeon for medical treatment and explained that he had been involved in an 'accident'. This could have been a motor accident or anything. No questions were asked. Buti received medical treatment, and food and water.

We then drove him home to Mamelodi much to the relief of his family, who were, by now, panic-stricken. So many people had disappeared at the hands of the security machinery and many didn't come back.

The family burst into tears when we brought Buti back home to them in Mamelodi.

The police were embarking on wholesale repression of any form of protest. In 1986, 10 years after the 1976 Soweto school uprising when the government proclaimed yet another state of emergency, Mamelodi was embraced under the national state of emergency declaration. The police felt that they could shoot anybody; arrest anybody; detain people without trial; and do exactly as they saw fit. There were many sad stories of homes that had been broken into, windows and doors being broken down or shot at, and even schoolchildren being chased out of their school.

I started the process of collecting a number of affidavits, or sworn declarations, from people who had suffered as a result of police brutality, or who had witnessed such brutality. I collected over 40 such declarations.

Having obtained them, I then sought an interview with the then Commissioner of Police, Brigadier Johan van Zyl. He was a frightening person. He had studied for a doctorate. His thesis for his doctorate was on communism. He believed that behind every bush or tree there lurked a communist.

At the interview, I handed him the affidavits. I told him that in my view these were complete violations of any human rights code which would operate in other countries. He attempted to justify the actions by saying that the police were defending themselves, which was surprising because the police were armed—the schoolchildren, however, were not. He tried to explain that our country was under a severe threat from the communist bloc; people who wanted to overturn the government and establish a communist regime.

I was not getting very far until I told him that I had made a copy of each sworn declaration and had sent a copy to Archbishop Desmond Tutu. This seemed to irritate him quite a bit but at least he sat up and took greater notice of what I was trying to tell him.

Some years later, having collected this evidence of the brutality, and having helped Buti on the streets after he had been kidnapped at night by the security police and beaten up by them, I received a call from a lawyer. He asked whether I could testify at a treason trial—more specifically, the Delmas Treason Trial.

Buti, along with several others, had been charged with treason. The State was applying its machinery against the accused to block them out of society for at least two years, along with their legal representatives. This was their ploy to gather as many people as they could and charge them with treason, tying them up in court for two to three years. They would of course make sure that the brightest defence lawyers would represent them, all being bound for the duration of the trial's proceedings. There were also witnesses.

The State would then charge them with treason, and the security police would provide evidence from their bank of information in the form of letters, news clippings and tape recordings. Laying on a judge and a prosecutor, in effect, it was a neat way to pin down some accused, and especially their counsel, for a long period. That meant Buti and his co-accused would in effect be fighting for their lives. Had they been found guilty of treason, there was the possibility of being sentenced to death.

Buti and the others were accused of treason. They were accused of plotting to bring down the State. In their case, they had not been acting in concert. They had been doing different things at different times, albeit aimed at promoting antigovernmental activities. Some had been promoting banned organisations and encouraging people to join them; others were trying to blow up fuel depots—and there had been one or two successes in that regard with the ANC masterminding raids while others were allegedly sowing unrest amongst the people in the townships.

There was no common act where they all joined together and acted in unison.

The government had introduced an interesting technical legal point. They were charged with treason because of a legal point known as 'common purpose'. Their common purpose was to overthrow the government, hence the charge of treason.

There were varying degrees of what the different people were trying to do. Some were more violent; some were more vocal—either way, it was obvious that there were more proactive individuals than others.

These differences in approach would lead to teams of defence lawyers being able to drive wedges between the arguments and witnesses of the State. This took time but that was what the State wanted: to keep them busy.

When the attorneys for the defence team called and asked whether I would give evidence, I hinted that I was busy running other projects for Get Ahead; trying to create jobs—but more particularly fighting for our survival by Wendy Richards and I spending 40% of our time trying to raise money from international corporations, embassies and foundations.

My plea was sympathetically heard. I was assured that I would not be involved for more than a day.

I was to provide evidence on two issues; the first being my encounter with Buti that morning in Church Street, Pretoria after his night of interrogation and beatings at the hands of the security police, and what I subsequently did with him, such as taking him to Nick de Villiers at the LRC so that he could recall the whole experience. Having gone to the district surgeon for medical treatment, I was also to mention that I did not take him to the police.

The second part of evidence I was to provide related to the affidavits and sworn declarations that I had collected from people of Mamelodi describing how they had suffered at the hands of the police, and what the police were currently doing to them. This element was required to describe the state of affairs that were prevailing in the country at the time, and how the police had become a law unto themselves and had very little regard for anybody's property, or even life.

Arthur Chaskalson was not in court that day. I was led by David Soggott, who, very much like Arthur, was also an eminent struggle fighter advocate. I was sworn in as a witness. David asked me to describe the events that morning in Church Street, Pretoria when Buti arrived and had thrown his arms around me.

I had carefully prepared notes to make sure that I would stick to the facts. I recounted the details carefully, mentioning how we went to Nick de Villiers at the LRC; then onto the medical surgeon. I was asked by David Soggott whether I had reported the matter to the police, and I replied simply: "No."

He didn't ask me why not.

He then asked me to describe some of the situations which had been prevailing in Mamelodi at the time. I described how we had collected various affidavits and I had brought copies to court. I was happy to make them available. David said it was not necessary. However, I described the brutality of the police and their total disregard for what I considered the ruling law.

This took an hour. That was all.

David sat down and said that he had no further questions to put to me.

This meant it was now the turn of the State attorney to start putting questions to me. He asked me to clarify a few of the practical details which may have been unclear. I did so.

He then asked me to repeat the answer to the earlier question of whether I had reported the beating up of Buti to the police. I replied that I had not.

He asked me: "Why not?"

I explained that in my view, it was the police who had perpetrated this act of violence, and my way of thinking was that it would not help Buti at all if I went back to the police.

"Why?" the State attorney enquired further.

I then said that in my opinion the police would either cover up the issue, or would not investigate the matter properly.

More especially, I said, a regular policeman at a normal charge office and who may in all conscience wish to do his duty, may be fearful of the security police, his own colleagues. I reminded the cross-examining State attorney that it was at the hands of the security police at Compol, that much-feared place, where Buti had been beaten up.

The State attorney attacked me vigorously. Did I have no faith in the police service? Did I not realise that the police were there to protect us? Were all police bad?

I tried to explain, carefully and without getting angry, that it would not have helped Buti's case at all because it was the police who had perpetrated the acts of violence; that indeed it was the Special Branch. And I then repeated that I could see no chance for Buti's case being properly investigated or brought to a satisfactory conclusion. Now at this stage the judge, Willem van der Merwe, barked at me: "But you are a lawyer. You are an officer of the court. You have had to administrate and practice the law. Do you not have faith in the policemen who uphold the law and maintain law and order?"

I replied that I had the greatest respect for the ordinary 'bobby on the beat'; the person who tried to prevent theft, drugs and what I described as the 'normal' crimes.

I tried to further explain that in my view, what had happened to Buti was abnormal. Here was an act of violence, a crime perpetrated by the very people who were supposed to keep law and order.

The debate raged on.

To and fro. Backwards and forward.

Sometimes questions coming from the State attorney; sometimes an angry rebuke from the judge.

The State attorney then changed tactics. He started asking me questions about why I was working in the black townships. "Did you not know that white people were not allowed to go to Soweto?" he asked. He wanted to know why I was the only white person on the Board of Directors of Get Ahead.

He then got to what he must have considered the axe with which he had to grind against me. He asked me why I worked for Archbishop Desmond

Tutu who, in his mind, was hostile because of his remarks against the government, and more particularly because of his call for sanctions against South Africa. Would sanctions not bring down the economy of the country? Was I not seeking to bring down the economy of the country by working with the Archbishop? Why was I working with Dr Motlana? Had I not read some of his vitriolic statements and pronouncements against the government? Did he not want chaos and anarchy?

I tried to explain that Get Ahead was a not-for-profit organisation. Its objectives were clearly stated: to create jobs for the unemployed, and provide opportunities for the unbanked, and the poor and needy.

I didn't make mention that some were main members of the ANC, while others were members of the PAC. Others might not belong to either party but were certainly opposed to the then government. I simply said that we had a board of directors who had different and varying views.

This did not satisfy the State attorney.

He seemed to suggest that because I was associating with people who were so hostile towards the government, I too, was an enemy of the State and hence my own country or homeland. In effect, I was guilty by association.

He never quite said this then but that was the atmosphere he created in the court.

I remember the words of Hugh Lewin when I first visited him in the political prison wing at the Pretoria Central Prison, long ago: "They will now consider you to be guilty as well—guilty by association."

After court on Tuesday afternoon, I was told that I would have to come back on Wednesday. The State had not yet finished with me, which was rather annoying because it meant I had to cancel all my appointments for that day.

On Wednesday morning, I arrived at the court early and was first in the courtroom. I had brought some work to do and needed to catch up on my reading. I sat in the witness box reading.

The next in the room was one of the security policemen who had been sitting next to the state attorney the afternoon before. I thought that I had noticed that he had passed bits of paper to the State attorney when he was cross-examining me. I was not entirely sure. We nodded to each other.

Next came the accused: Buti, Peter Maluleka, and the others. I nodded to them but then gave them the thumbs-up sign.

Normally, this would be a harmless thing to do and would signify 'good luck'. Pilots do it as they are about to take off. Parking attendants give the sign when they alert a driver that the car is in the right place.

Yet, the thumbs-up gesture was a very special one. It was the ANC sign for unity.

Having given a thumbs-up to the accused, they responded almost in unison, and automatically. The response to the thumbs-up sign was immediate from all.

Not a word passed between us; only acknowledgement and the reciprocating of the thumbs-up sign.

The State attorney continued with his cross-examination.

Why had I not gone to the police? And so, we went over the same points again. I suppose that he was trying to make me change my story. Perhaps this should make me an unreliable witness. This was the State attempting to tie down the accused and their counsel for years.

We continued with our verbal battles. Around and around we went.

Immediately after the tea break, the State attorney asked if I was the first in the courtroom, to which I replied affirmatively.

"Were you here when the accused were brought into court?" he questioned.

"Yes," I replied.

"And when they walked in did you give them any particular hand sign?" the State attorney pressed.

Yes, I said again, telling him I gave them a good luck sign. I gave them the thumbs-up sign.

This then led the State attorney to cross-examine me for an hour on whether I knew that the thumbs-up sign was the recognised greeting of the ANC.

I tried to dodge the issue by explaining that amongst township people, hand signs were very important.

Each soccer club, for example, had its own particular finger raising or finger waiving sign. The two fingers in a 'V', or the peace sign, was well-known as the Kaizer Chiefs soccer club sign. One finger pointing upwards with the thumb at a right angle is the Mamelodi Sundowns' sign. Crossed forearms was the Orlando Pirates sign.

There were also different signs if you wanted to catch taxis. A raised index finger meant that you were going to town. A finger pointed horizontally signified that you wish to get a taxi ride around the townships of Soweto or wherever you were standing.

The State attorney did not accept this. He believed that I was now promoting matters to do with the ANC by giving the accused a thumbs-up sign.

We argued on and on.

He was of course correct: I had given the sign but was not prepared to admit that this was any way of promoting the aims and objectives of a banned political organisation.

During the lunchtime break, I pondered in amazement at how much time and effort was being spent on what I considered to be trivial matters. In my view, these were trivial in light of the greater picture: the charges of treason. If the accused were unsuccessful, this could lead to a death sentence.

I resolved to do my best—I would not let the team down.

The cross-examination was eventually concluded that afternoon. At the end of that second day, I was told that I had to come back the next day. This meant that I had to cancel all my arrangements for yet another day. When I got home, I was absolutely exhausted. I went to bed at 6:00pm that night. The whole day of cross-examination in the witness box had totally drained me.

It was on the third day in the witness box that I let rip a bit. I lost a little bit of control and delivered a tongue lashing.

The State attorney was at it again. The security policeman had been passing him pieces of information while he was cross-examining me. I was asked if I visited the political prisoners at the Pretoria Central Prison. "Yes," I replied. "But that was nearly 20 years ago." Here they were coming with their guilty by association attack again!

Was it not the duty of the police to maintain law and order in the community, I was asked.

"Yes," I replied.

"Why then did you not take Buti to the police and report his having been beaten up?" the State prosecution probed. This must have been the seventh or eighth time in three days that we were now back on this track.

I replied, as I always had, because it was the police who had beaten up Buti.

I was being put on trial as the accused—and there was no doubt about it! Fear gripped that courtroom. One bad slip, and the accused would be convicted.

Having given my verbal testimony on Tuesday, I was eventually released on Friday morning—three days in the witness box. No wonder Dr Motlana had told how the State was using trumped up court cases as a means of tying down many opponents of the State, and the cleverest lawyers. Block them out for years.

Eventually, when the court adjourned and I was told that I no longer had to come back, I was about to ask defence counsel leader David whether I had managed OK.

The accused however gave me the answer. As I left, they gleefully turned towards me and gave the thumbs-up sign then clapped their hands very appreciably before being led down to the cells by the police.

The State asked for an adjournment to get more witnesses. Another stalling tactic. However, it was in that time when the tides of change arrived in South Africa, and the trial was completely turned on its head, eventually coming to an end in December 1988. Almost a year later, United Democratic Front members won a Supreme Court of Appeal ruling that saw 11 of the accused released from jail.

The newly-elected president of the country, F.W. de Klerk, then announced on 2 February 1990, that he would revoke all banning legislation and regulations. He would abolish those laws that had banned parties like the ANC and PAC, and others. All political prisoners would be released, and their charges immediately dropped, which covered Buti and his co-accused. Steps would be taken to adopt a new constitution giving universal franchise for all, and a general election would be held to encompass people of all races.

Fantastic! Unbelievable!

Buti and his co-accused were released and all charges were dropped.

What made President F.W. de Klerk do that without a mandate from his white electorate? No debate in Parliament between the white representatives? Had the president suffered a 'Road to Damascus' moment? The questions raged.

After meeting F.W. de Klerk as a young man, when he joined my father's law firm to serve his articles of clerkship to become admitted as an attorney, he was very kind to me over the years. He invited me for coffee in Parliament while still a backbencher. I also met with him in his Plattekloof office when he became deputy president, doing some trademark work for him.

The amazing thing for me was that he carried with him the whole electorate. The history of white political events was so often tainted with anger, stormy meetings, hurling abuse, and throwing chairs at each other at heated meetings. But here he was, taking the whole country in his hands, white and black. A remarkable man. A remarkable turn of events.

At the back of my mind was the realisation that the political heat had brought about the changes that were happening around us. The waves of sanctions, and disinvestment were starting to hurt. South Africa had been dubbed the polecat of the world. Boycotts were cutting into our financial and living ways. Sports boycotts were felt by all. And the person who had started all the boycotts was the Archbishop.

23 ~ The Big Day

We will never forget the day of 11 February 1990. It is one of those days to be remembered, for always. Much like when people ask, where were you standing when JFK was assassinated? Or, where were you on 9/11 when the Twin Towers fell?

For South Africans, we have some days to be remembered. Such as 16 June 1976, when the Soweto children erupted against the government and its planned education policy.

For us, 11 February 1990 was magic. It was the day that Nelson Mandela was released from prison after 27 years behind bars.

Generally, the country accepted these political announcements, and proposed changes, without major turmoil. That was indeed surprising. Yes. There were some hiccups. Like, who can forget the smashing of the glass doors at the World Trade Centre in Kempton Park, later, when angry Afrikaans agitators drove a military vehicle into the doors of the building, when the peace process was in progress?

Or the assassination of veteran struggle hero, Chris Hani? So sad. So unnecessary.

South Africa's history is riddled with conflict stories like the Boer War and the Rand Rebellion. Similarly, the tensions between the white parties, when the throwing of chairs at each other at political meetings was the norm. South Africans can get very hot under the collar!

But no. It was a peaceful transition. The foreign press came in droves in 1990, and again, when the 1994 election took place. Back then, they spoke of revolt and bloody conflict. They were like vultures hovering for the fall and collapse. It didn't happen. That might have been because of the leaders who were involved then—people like Archbishop Tutu, President F.W. de Klerk and President Nelson Mandela. In my view, all three deserved their Nobel Peace Prizes.

For a bit of lightheartedness, in 1994, Get Ahead's board agreed to open a shebeen in the middle of Johannesburg. This was not a legitimate bar. On the contrary, we did everything an illegal shebeen queen would do. Not obey the law! We even had a Soweto jazz band perform called the Elite Swingsters. Good fun. This taste of Soweto, right in the middle of Johannesburg was a hit. Then I received a call from London, from Prudence Scarlett on behalf of the Commonwealth Society. She explained that now that South Africa would be re-admitted to the Commonwealth, there was to be a big welcoming ceremony at Westminster Abbey, London, followed by a garden party at Buckingham Palace. Archbishop Tutu would be officiating, but she wanted the Soweto jazz band to perform. The board was happy with this publicity, and Wendy Richards was superb in taking the band all the way to the Abbey and garden party. She also produced a brochure telling about Get Ahead and a list of donors who had supported our company—it is attached as Annexure 1. I was pleasantly surprised at how the numbers had grown. I also attach as Annexure 2, the names of all those who had worked for Get Ahead. I sadly cannot recall all the names, and I am sure that Wendy and I have omitted some.

That Sunday morning in February 1990 was so special. Archbishop Tutu and his wife, Leah, had invited us to Soweto for the early christening of their grandson, Lizo Tutu, the son of Trevor and Zanele. The service was held at the Holy Cross Church, very near to the Tutus' Soweto home. As we drove into Soweto, the streets were quiet. Not very many people around. Marianne waved happily to a newspaper vendor. He waved back shouting: "Viva Mandela! Viva de Klerk!"

That created the right atmosphere and got me thinking about some of our leaders. Like Dr Motlana, and his angry attitude towards the former government. And when he castigated the government for giving him a passport valid for only five days, and mentioning only one country, Egypt, to enable him to be the guest speaker at a UN health convention. Dr Albertina Luthuli and her daughter Lungile had reminded me of how her father, Dr Albert Luthuli had been delayed for a year to allow him to receive his Nobel Peace Prize, in Oslo. And of course, the Arch himself, showing the world his own limited passport, and the clear wording on his passport, describing his nationality as being "unknown". The Arch spoke angrily. In fact, during those 14 years of working in Soweto for the Arch, followed by a further 17 years of being on the Board of the Desmond & Leah Tutu Legacy Foundation, I only saw the Arch getting angry twice. Once to express anger against the former apartheid regime. The other was in 2011 against the ANC-led government when they refused to grant a visa to enable the Dalai Lama to give the Annual Tutu Memorial Peace Lecture on Tutu's 80th birthday. Marianne and I were in the Cape Town cathedral to celebrate his 80th birthday, and just before the commencement of the Cathedral service, the Arch left his seat near the pulpit to walk into the congregation to give a big bear hug to the president—to amend the soured relationship. That embrace, in the full view of the TV cameras, says so much for reconciliation.

On that morning in February 1990, I pondered about leaving Marianne and our children to work in Soweto when better financial opportunities had beckoned. They never murmured a word. I am so grateful to them.

The happy and loud greeting of the "Viva!" by the happy newspaper vendor changed all that in an instant.

At the church, the place was packed. Buzzing with excitement. A whole press brigade was there. Cameras, notebooks, interviews. Even inside the church, the paparazzi blocked the front pews.

Anglican churches have a nice tradition during each service. You shake hands with your neighbour, look each other in the eye, and say: "Peace be with you." This is how it is done in the white parishes. Very demurely. Very politely.

The Holy Cross Church in Soweto was different. When it came to the passing of the peace, the congregation started singing. Thumping their bibles in unison. Loudly. Clapping hands. In gratitude. And then they took to the aisles to dance and weave about. The gaiety was a far cry from the little white service.

Then the Arch galloped down from the pulpit and offered to dance with Marianne. She is a very good dancer, and they whirled around the aisles, up to the pulpit, laughing all the way. The press brigade loved it. Following them around with their cameras over their shoulders, grabbing every bite of news for the international newswires.

My friend van Zyl Slabbert, the former leader of the Progressive Party, was lecturing at All Souls College, in Oxford. He called that night laughingly saying: "Hey! Hold on! They haven't quite scrapped the Group Areas Act. You cannot dance across the colour bar just yet!" The country was ablaze with happiness.

We went to the nearby Tutu home for an early lunch and coffee. Then the Arch dashed off to catch a private jet to Cape Town to be there in the reception group to greet Nelson Mandela as he and Winnie came out of the gate. What an explosion. South Africa and the whole world were watching.

That is why that day is so very special. Don't forget that date.

So much has been written about Mandela—the accolades showered on him. What a man. I only want to touch on a few points about him.

While in Soweto, I mused to myself; I might be a candidate for being arrested but for my thoughts, not actions. I must have been a person who wanted to throw Molotov cocktails, or hand-held glass bombs, at the government and Special Branch, however, Mr Mandela showed us a better way. One of peace. The strength of his character was demonstrated when, years later, he met face-to-face with Dr Percy Yutar, the man who urged the judge during the Rivonia Trial to sentence Mandela to life imprisonment on a charge of sabotage, and not treason, which would mean death. This followed the now-famous *I am prepared to die* speech delivered over the course of three hours.

Can you imagine the vitriol in court surrounding this case? The smearing, scoffing, the belittling from the bar that Dr Yutar would have faced?

After his release, Mr Mandela had a peaceful cup of coffee with Dr Yutar.

He then went further. He had coffee with Mrs Betsie Verwoerd, the widow of the former Prime Minister, Hendrik Verwoerd, the architect of all hated apartheid laws. The whites, especially former supporters, were amazed. Such conciliation. What a shining example!

In all the years I was fortunate to meet and act for him, I only saw Mr Mandela get angry, once. He often had reason to do that, like when a scaly, white South African had fled from the country and was hiding in Brisbane, Australia, and had registered the domain name NelsonMandela.com.

Or again, when one of the political parties in Brazil, during a referendum on the principle of private people carrying guns, had an election poster stating that "Freedom fighter Nelson Mandela always carried a gun." Nothing could have been further from the truth.

And I wondered whether Mr Mandela showed fear. Anger with the racist government—yes. Or possibly retribution. Who can blame him for such thoughts? But, did he possibly smile when he was eventually caught by the security police after they found him dressed up as a chauffeur for a so-called white employer? He did not show any fear when he spoke from the dock in his treason trial, which imprisoned him for life. No. He stood up to the judge when making his poignant speech on human rights.

I started this book by referring to fear. My own fear. But surprisingly I never experienced fear from any black person. Even when standing on the pavement as the young men ran past me singing struggle songs after a funeral. Or when I saw burning tyres blocking the road against the police.

On the contrary, I was welcomed very courteously in every house I visited. Often, I was offered water, or tea. Like Beauty Sithole, the cleaning lady who invited me into her tin house shanty. Or Sifiso Ncgobo and his mother welcoming our international rugby visitors.

But the fear was there. Often. I often felt petrified. Like when visiting the security police at their head office in John Vorster Square. Or when they descended on us and raided seven of our offices at the same time, and my hands started shaking.

The fear was there but created by whites in authority and based on their own fear that they believed must also be felt by others. This fuelled a system that the whole world, and many of us, despised.

But it was a marvellous experience. In my view, no white person has had such a rich life.

As a lawyer, I was reminded of that conversation many years ago with Labour Party backbencher, Elwyn Lloyd, later to become UK Chancellor, when he doubted my view that South Africa should have any Nuremburg Trials, which followed World War II. No. President Nelson Mandela took a different direction. He instituted the Truth and Reconciliation Commission (TRC) chaired by Archbishop Tutu, and Alex Boraine. I remember how people cried in court when giving their testimony, or when others had come forward to describe their acts of aggression against people who revolted against the State. In particular, the TRC report covering police brutality in the township of Mamelodi went much further than the affidavits that I handed to the security police. The TRC's process was a first, copied later by other governments around the world.

Without a doubt, Nelson Mandela was a truly great man.

Annexure 1 – Get Ahead donor list

GETAHEAD FOUNDATION
(A Non-Profit Company)

227 Minnaar Street
(near Paul Kruger Street)
PRETORIA

Offices in the following centres:

Acornhoek
Atteridgeville
Cape Town

Durban
East London
Ga-Rankuwa
Katlehong

Mamelodi
Pietermaritzburg
Port Elizabeth

Sebokeng
Soweto
Tembisa
Uitenhage

WRITE TO:
P.O. Box 3776
Pretoria
0001

Tel: (012) 320-6530
Fax No: (012) 320 8288

UPDATED DONOR LIST

ABSA GOLDEN HEART TRUST
ADCOCK INGRAM LIMITED
AECI LIMITED
AFROX LIMITED
AI INSURANCE COMPANY LIMITED
AMREL AMALGAMATED RETAIL LIMITED
ANGLO ALPHA LIMITED
ANGLO AMERICAN CHAIRMAN'S FUND
ANGLOVAAL GROUP EDUCATIONAL TRUST
AUSTRALIAN EMBASSY
AUSTRIAN DEVELOPMENT CO-OPERATION
BARING FOUNDATION
BASF SOUTH AFRICA (PTY) LTD
BATEMAN LIMITED, EDWARD L
BIDVEST CHAIRMANS FUND
BKS INCORPORATED
BMW (SOUTH AFRICA) (PTY) LTD
BOARD OF EXECUTORS
BORDEN FOODS (PTY) LTD
CADBURY SCHWEPPES (SOUTH AFRICA) LIMITED
CALTEX OIL (SA) (PTY) LTD
CANADIAN BLACK BUSINESS SA (CABBSA)
CAXTON LIMITED
CHASE MANHATTAN BANK
CHEMICAL SERVICES LIMITED
CITIBANK
CITY OF PIETERMARITZBURG
CITY PLANNERS DEPARTMENT - PIETERMARITZBURG
COCA COLA SOUTHERN AFRICA (PTY) LTD
COLLINS REV. JTOB
CREDA PRESS (PTY) LTD
CUDAHY FUND, PATRICK & ANNA
CUMMINS CORPORATION
DAVID BROWN GEAR INDUSTRIES (PTY) LIMITED
DEUTSCHE GESELLSCHAFT FUR TECHNISCHE ZUSAMMENARBEIT (GTZ)
DORBYL LIMITED
DOUGLAS MURRAY TRUST
DU PONT DE NEMOURS INTERNATIONAL
DURBAN CORPORATION
ESKOM
FAURE MR ABE
FILPRO (PTY) LTD
FIRST NATIONAL BANK LIMITED
FISCHER, MS SUSAN
FLUOR SOUTH AFRICA
FOODCORP LIMITED
FOSCHINI GROUP (PTY) LTD
FRENCH EMBASSY
GATSBY CHARITABLE FOUNDATION
GEARMAX (PTY) LTD
GIBSON MR P & A
GILLETTE SOUTH AFRICA LTD
GLASS SOUTH AFRICA (PTY) LTD
GORDON GRAY TRUST
GRINDROD (PTY) LTD
GROUP FIVE CORPORATE SERVICES (PTY) LTD

GTZ GEFE
H.J. HEINZ COMPANY FOUNDATION
HALL MR COLIN
HI-PERFORMANCE SYSTEMS (PTY) LTD
HUDACO TRADING LIMITED
HULETT ALUMINIUM (PTY) LTD
HUNT LEUCHARS & HEPBURN HOLDINGS LTD
IN-AS-MUCH
INDEPENDENT NEWSPAPER GROUP
INDUSTRIAL DEVELOPMENT CORPORATION OF SOUTH AFRICA
INTERNATIONAL BUSINESS MACHINES (IBM)
INTERNATIONAL COMPUTERS (SOUTH AFRICA) (PTY) LTD
INTERNATIONAL ENTERPRISE FOUNDATION OF GENEVA
ISCOR LIMITED
ITHUBA TRUST
JAFF & COMPANY LIMITED
JAPANESE GOVERNMENT
JH ISAACS GROUP
JOHANNESBURG-CONSOLIDATED INVESTMENT COMPANY LIMITED
JOHN DEERE
JP MORGAN & CO
KANGRA FOUNDATION
KELLOGG CO OF SA
KODAK (SOUTH AFRICA) (PTY) LTD
KONRAD ADENAUR
LEHRMAN, RONALD J
LIBERTY LIFE FOUNDATION
LINTAS (PTY) LTD
LONRHO MANAGEMENT SERVICES (PTY) LTD
3M (SOUTH AFRICA) (PTY) LTD
MACSTEEL CORPORATE SERVICES (PTY) LTD
MARSHALLS GROUP LTD
MASKEW MILLER LONGMAN (PTY) LTD
MASONITE (AFRICA) LIMITED
MAYOR OF SANDTON - B W BURNS
MCCARTHY RETAIL LTD
MCINTOSH MR DEREK
MERCK & CO
MICHIGAN EDUCATION ASSOCIATION
MILLS MR P V
MURRAY & ROBERTS
NAMPAK MANAGEMENT SERVICES
NATAL WITNESS
NATIONAL BEVERAGES SERVICES (PTY) LTD
NEDCOR COMMUNITY DEVELOPMENT FUND
NESTLE (SOUTH AFRICA) (PTY) LTD
NORTHERN FOODS
NORWICH LIFE SOUTH AFRICA LTD
ORAL B LABORATORIES (SA) (PTY) LTD
OTIS ELEVATOR COMPANY LIMITED
PEP STORES LTD
PETERSON A H, ESTATE OF
PHG CADBURY CHARITABLE TRUST
PIETERMARITZBURG CHAMBER OF COMMERCE & INDUSTRY

PREMIER FOOD SOCIAL INVESTMENT COUNCIL
PRICE FORBES GROUP
PROCTOR & GAMBLE SA (PTY) LTD
PROTEA ASSURANCE
R & B MCDONALD SEEDS
RECKITT & COLMAN
ROLIN M GERSTACKER FOUNDATION
ROMATEX LIMITED
ROSE EJB CHARITABLE TRUST
ROSE MR & MRS J
SA AIRWAYS
SANLAM
SASOL LIMITED
SCHUDT MR ANNAEUS
SEAGRAM JE
SEARDEL INVESTMENT CORPORATION LIMITED
SIEMENS
SILTEK
SOMTA TOOLS (PTY) LTD
SOUTH AFRICAN BREWERIES
SOUTHERN AFRICAN TRADE ASSOCIATION
SOUTHERN LIFE FOUNDATION
STANDARD BANK FOUNDATION
STUCKEN & CO (PTY) LTD
SUN INTERNATIONAL
SUNCRUSH LIMITED
SUTHERLAND JB ESTATE OF
SWISS CONTACT
T & N HOLDINGS LIMITED
TEC-WE-GWILL WOMENS INSTITUTE
TEMPLESMAN MAURICE
TIAS
TIMES MEDIA LIMITED
TIOXIDE SOUTHERN AFRICA (PTY) LTD
TOPIC STORES (PTY) LTD
TOTAL SOUTH AFRICA (PTY) LTD
TR SMALLER COMPANIES INVESTMENT TRUST
TRENCOR
TRUWORTHS LIMITED
TUPPERWARE
TUSK MUSIC COMPANY (PTY) LTD
UMGENI WATER
UNILEVER (SA) (PTY) LTD
UNITED INTERNATIONAL PICTURES
UNITED STATES AGENCY FOR INTERNATIONAL DEVELOPMENT (USAID)
UNIVERSITY OF CAPE TOWN (DEPT. OF PHARMACOLOGY)
UPJOHN (PTY) LTD
US FUND FOR LEADERSHIP (CHARLES STETSON)
VANTAGE PENSION ADMINISTRATORS (PTY) LTD
W K KELLOGG FOUNDATION
WOOLWORTHS (PTY) LTD
WYSELIOT CHARITABLE TRUST

DIRECTORS : Dr Nthato Motlana (Chairman), Snowy Mashigo, Dikgang Moseneke, Daphne Motsepe, Percy Nkuna, Philip Ramakotya, Sizwe Tati, Archbishop Desmond Tutu, Ismail Skosana and Don MacRobert (Managing)

Annexure 2 – List of workers

Get Ahead board members

South Africa
Dr Nthato Motlana (Chairman)
Archbishop Desmond Tutu
Judge Dikgang Moseneke
Thubs Mathabatha
Snowy Mashigo
Thabo Lesolang
Jimmy Sojane
Israel Skosana
Sizwe Tati
Daphne Motsepe
Mthunzi Pupuma
Percy Nkuna

USA
Dr Nthato Motlana
Senator Edward Kennedy
Walter Carrington
David Miller
Joe MacMahon
Peter Graves
William Hayden
Sizwe Tati
Daniel Rose
Mpho Tutu
Maurice Templesman
Anne McFarren

Get Ahead heroes

Gilbert Xaba
Mike Quawa
Dudley Mekgoe
Zipora Malaudi
Martha Magashwa
Pam Taylor
Jenny Williams
John de Wit
Glaudine Kruger
Price Mabula
Japie Moropa
Pro Molefe
John Nkosi
Wendy Richards
Atwell Msauli
Joe Ramangoa
Margie Ramangoa
Yvonne Radinkue
Daphne Motsepe
Lindi Mtimkulu
Israel Skosana
Mthunzi Pupuma
Eric Tseane
Peter Magano
Peggy Shabangu
Joe Letholi

Djundju Mathibe
Dave Sellick
Nelson Phiri
Wendy Bloy
Julia Mothepe
Betty Slater
Doke Monegi
Trevor Tutu
Philemon Machene
Ora Joubert
Jenny Walters
Joyce Sithole
Mam Lizzie
Gladys Ngwenya
Vanessa van Niekerk
Marina Clarke
Koketso Moseneke
Peter Maluleke
Thabo Makgoba
Leslie Matlasaine
Wendy Matselane
Astrid Ludin
Zweli Zondozeli
Thalia Moseneke
Craig Churchill
Sheila Valentini